# PRIMER contents

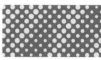

# A SEA WITHOUT A SHORE

There is an old hymn that wonderfully captures the theme and the goal of this issue of *Primer*:

*How great a being, Lord, is thine,*
*which doth all beings keep!*
*Thy knowledge is the only line*
*to sound so vast a deep.*
*Thou art a sea without a shore,*
*a sun without a sphere;*
*thy time is now and evermore,*
*thy place is everywhere.*

How Shall I Sing That Majesty? by John Mason.

Our theme is God himself. We plan to marvel at who he is. As his people, it ought to be the most natural and wonderful thing to do. And one thing I love about that hymn is the way it helps us to marvel mostly in words of one syllable. It is possible to speak simply and deeply of God.

And yet, there are some challenges I've been wrestling with:

First, there is so much to say! For that reason we have decided to give two issues of *Primer* to this topic. In this issue we will be looking at some of the traditional attributes of God. In the next issue we'll be thinking about the three persons of God – the Father, Son and Holy Spirit – who share those attributes.

For a glimpse of what's in store, see the inside back cover.

Second, there is the question of where to start. We believe in one God eternally existing in three persons. So do you start with what unites them as one God or what distinguishes them as three persons? In essence, I don't think it matters so long as you hold them together. As the early church theologian Gregory of Nazianzus once said, "No sooner do I conceive of the One than I am illumined by the splendour of the Three; no sooner do I distinguish Them than I am carried back to the One." Because this issue of *Primer* emphasises the *One*, I suppose that Gregory is simply telling you to buy the next issue as well ;-)

From Oration 40, 'On Holy Baptism.'

Third, there is considerable debate today about the doctrine of God. For centuries, the historic confessions of the church reflect what is now known as *classical theism*. Take for example, the first of the Church of England's 39 articles:

> *There is but one living and true God, everlasting, without body, parts, or passions; of infinite power, wisdom, and goodness; the Maker, and Preserver of all things both visible and invisible.*

The words are still mostly of one or two syllables, and there are some familiar words in there: *power*, *wisdom* and *goodness*. But there are also strange words: *without parts, or passions*. They reflect a strong and enduring thought in theology that God is utterly different to us. He is not created; he does not change; he is not bound by time or space. Over many centuries, the vocabulary of classical theism emerged to articulate and defend these things, speaking of the *aseity* and *simplicity* and *impassibility* of God.

See also the beginning of the *Westminster Confession of Faith*'s statement regarding God: "*There is but one only, living, and true God: who is infinite in being and perfection, a most pure spirit, invisible, without body, parts, or passions, immutable, immense, eternal, incomprehensible, almighty, most wise, most holy, most free, most absolute…*"

On the other hand, though, the 20th century saw a number of movements such as *process theology* or *open theism* which strongly opposed the classical doctrine of God and wanted to make God more like us. Especially in a post-Holocaust culture, it proved appealing to speak of God sharing in the suffering of his world, and, in a post-modern culture suspicious of authority, to describe God as involved in the give-and-take and vulnerability of relationships.

Evangelicals rejected both of those movements because of their clear denial of what Scripture teaches about God's sovereignty and unchanging character. Without needing to invoke the full weight of the classical doctrine of God, they clearly sit outside the bounds of something like the FIEC Statement of Faith on the doctrine of God:

> *There is one God, who exists eternally in three distinct but equal persons: the Father, the Son, and the Holy Spirit. God is unchangeable in his holiness, justice, wisdom and love. He is the almighty Creator; Saviour and Judge who sustains and governs all things according to his sovereign will for his own glory.*

Where the debate continues, however, is whether the classical doctrine of God is the best account of who God is and how Scripture describes him to us? If you say "no" to trends like process theology or open theism should you also say "yes" to classical theism? Does the Bible invite us or require us to speak about God's aseity, impassibility and so on?

I hope that these questions seem inherently important. We are trying to speak responsibly about God in light of what he has revealed about himself. There is no greater privilege and there is no greater responsibility. But they aren't easy questions to answer for a number of reasons:

- Many of us are simply unfamiliar with the classical doctrine of God, and as we have seen, it involves learning some new terms and not all of them of one syllable. For that reason we have designed this issue of *Primer* to be an introduction to the classical doctrine of God. We have worked hard to provide an accessible and reliable guide, but there's some careful thinking to do here, so: phone off, kettle on...

- Our churchmanship plays a role here. The classical doctrine of God is enjoying a significant revival at the moment, especially amongst Anglicans and Presbyterians for whom it forms part of their confessional standards. Likewise, Baptists who subscribe to the 1689 *Baptist Confession of Faith* are understandably highlighting it as part of their theological heritage. Those of us who are less clearly tied to a confessional tradition may not be formally required to assent to this teaching, but we will surely want to reflect on these things and learn all we can.

- We also need to be alert to a number of assumptions that will affect how we answer the question. Some of us, for example, will put more weight on tradition than others, when it comes to theology. That means that we will feel different degrees of anxiety about innovating or contradicting historical theology. Relatedly, some of us will be suspicious that theologians of every age are imposing some kind of foreign framework on Scripture. In the area of the doctrine of God, there is the added concern

**WE HAVE DESIGNED THIS ISSUE OF PRIMER TO BE AN INTRODUCTION TO THE CLASSICAL DOCTRINE OF GOD**

that our theology has borrowed from various streams of Greek philosophy. Some of us, therefore, rightly or wrongly, are on our guard against theological geeks bearing gifts.

- Finally, we should not ignore our own sinfulness. You may have heard the old quip that "God created man in his own image and man, being a gentleman, returned the favour." The point is this: as we come to this issue of *Primer* we need to know that we all cherish all kinds of ideas about God that are wrong. In some instances, that is because we are finite creatures who only have created realities with which to compare and describe an infinite Creator. But it is also true to say that in some cases we think wrongly about God because we *want* to think wrongly about God. We'd prefer a more detached and domesticated God, "there if you wish for him, like a book on a shelf." Or a God who needs me and with whom I can negotiate. A God with a back to be scratched so that he, in turn, can scratch mine.

Variously attributed to Voltaire, Rousseau, and Mark Twain.

C. S. Lewis, *Miracles* (Glasgow: Fontana, 1976), 97.

With those things in mind, let me introduce you to *Primer* issue 08. We begin by addressing some of the frequently asked questions about the classical doctrine of God: isn't the Bible more interested in teaching us about what God has done than who he is? Even if it is interested in that, has the church got it right? Graham Shearer guides us through those questions, helping us to see that a commitment to Scripture as God's word has important implications for how we think about God.

Next we introduce you to three of the major but less well-known classical attributes of God. Gerald Bray gives us an overview of God's aseity (I won't spoil the surprise!). Nick Tucker guides us through our historical text from one of the church's A-Team, and introduces us to God's simplicity. And then Chris Stead helps us understand why we would ever speak about God as 'without passions' and why that could be very good news indeed. Importantly, Chris applies this traditional doctrine of God to pastoral life and the final two articles continue in that vein. Sam Bostock talks us through his recent sermons on Exodus, showing how a grasp of theology nourishes Bible reading and teaching. And finally, Matt Lillicrap reflects on the difference our doctrine of God makes in the highs and lows of ministry.

I trust it goes without saying that this is not the final word on the doctrine of God! But I do hope that these articles help us to engage afresh with Scripture and to appreciate centuries of Christian reflection. Look out for additional resources at *PrimerHQ.com* and for issue 09 on the Trinity in November 2019...

**DAVID SHAW** is the Editor of *Primer*. He is part-time Theological Adviser for FIEC and part-time lecturer in New Testament and Greek at Oak Hill College, London. He's married to Jo and they have four children.

 **@_david_shaw**

**GRAHAM SHEARER** is the Associate Pastor of East London Tabernacle Baptist Church. He lives in Hackney with his wife, Katherine, and their three children. He blogs at *gjshearer.wordpress.com*

🐦 *@GJShearer*

Beholding the invisible God in the pages of Scripture

**Early on in my training for Christian ministry, I was taught that the Bible was a story and that the key element to focus on, therefore, was the plot; the grand narrative from the Garden to the City. As a result, the questions that occupied much of Christian theology in the past (e.g. whether God is divisible, whether he can change) were peripheral at best. The focus of the Bible is on what God has *done*; his acts, not his being.**

At the time, this seemed to be self-evidently true. Listening to a steady diet of expository preaching, my attention was drawn to the great works of redemption-history, and it seemed to make very little difference how I understood God's relation to time or whether he could change – and I don't think I ever heard the strange idea that God was 'simple.' Perhaps my experience was unusual, but my suspicion is that much of evangelicalism considers the doctrine of God to be, as I once heard said, "there in the Bible, but not particularly important." Others are more critical still, viewing the traditional doctrine as little more than Greek philosophy in Christian clothes.

My thinking began to change when I attended a training day on Augustine's *Confessions*. On the one hand, like so many, I resonated with Augustine's account of his spiritual journey and yet, on the other, I was perplexed by the way Augustine places the unchanging and perfect nature of God front and centre in his reflections upon the spiritual life. For instance, in his opening pages Augustine writes,

*Confessions,*
*I.iv*

NB. Here Augustine is relying on a Latin translation of Job, which is why this doesn't match our English translations.

*Who then are you, my God? ... Most high, utterly good, utterly powerful, most omnipotent, most merciful and most just, deeply hidden yet most intimately present, perfection of both beauty and strength, stable and incomprehensible, immutable and yet changing all things, never new, never old, making everything new and 'leading' the proud 'to be old without their knowledge' (Job 9:5); always active, always in repose, gathering to yourself but not in need, supporting and filling and protecting, creating and nurturing and bringing to maturity, searching even though to you nothing is lacking: you love without burning, you are jealous in a way that is free of anxiety, you 'repent' (Gen 6:6) without the pain of regret, you are wrathful and remain tranquil. You will a change without any change in your design. You recover what you find, yet have never lost. Never in any need, you rejoice in your gains (Luke 15:7); you are never greedy, yet you require interest (Matt 25:27). We pay you more than you require so as to make you our debtor, yet who has anything which does not belong to you? (1 Cor 4:7). You pay off debts, though owing nothing to anyone; you cancel debts and incur no loss.*

It is perhaps best summarised by the Westminster Confession of Faith (WCF), which states *"There is but one only living and true God, who is infinite in being and perfection, a most pure spirit, invisible, without body, parts, or passions, immutable, immense, eternal, incomprehensible, almighty, most wise, most holy, most free, most absolute."* WCF II.i.

Augustine's understanding of God has sometimes been called *classical theism* reflecting the fact that it has been the consensus position of the church throughout its history. Key figures as diverse as...

Athanasius, (4th century bishop of Alexandria in Egypt)

the Cappadocian Fathers, (two brothers: Basil the Great & Gregory of Nyssa, and their friend Gregory of Nazianzus – 4th century bishops in what is now Turkey)

Anselm, (11-12th century medieval theologian and archbishop – see an extract from one of his works on page 30)

Thomas Aquinas, (13th century Italian preacher and theologian)

John Calvin, (16th century French pastor and reformer)

John Owen (17th century English pastor and theologian)

and Herman Bavinck (19th-20th century Dutch theologian)

Including the 39 Articles, the Belgic Confession, and Westminster, Savoy and Second London Baptist Confessions.

...would all have recognised Augustine's understanding as their own and it is reflected in the confessions of the English and European Reformation. Yet, to me, it was largely new and unfamiliar and raised significant questions.

- First, is any of this really the focus of the Scriptures or is it the preoccupation of abstract philosophising owing more to Plato and Aristotle than to Jesus and Paul?

- Second, if the Scriptures are concerned to teach about God's essence, is this really what they teach? How does the idea that God is unchangeable fit with all the texts that speak of God changing in one way or another? Didn't God change when the Son became a man?

My guess is that many contemporary British evangelicals share these questions and hesitations about the classical doctrine of God, and this is why our constituency tends to either neglect or modify it so that it plays a much smaller part in our spiritual lives than it did for

Augustine and the Reformers. In this article, then, I want to answer the question of whether classical theism is compatible with the revelation of God in Scripture and in Christ and, if it is, what that means for how we understand Scripture and Christ himself.

## one. Is the Doctrine of God a Biblical Concern?

We need to begin with this question: do the Scriptures really push us to consider God's nature or is it a concern foreign to the Bible's main concern of narrating God's redemption of humanity in Christ? Discussions of God's simplicity, his 'pure actuality', the distinction between person and nature, and so on, do not seem to spring naturally from the biblical text for many modern readers. There are, however, at least three points which might be raised in response to this question which explain why, for most of church history, believers reading the Scriptures have been drawn to reflect upon God's nature.

First, while the bulk of Scripture narrates or reflects upon God's actions in time and space, there are times when the vocabulary of Scripture forces us to consider what it means for God to be God. The most obvious, and widespread, is the use of the word 'God' (*elohim* in Hebrew or *theos* in Greek) throughout the Scriptures. What does the writer have in mind when he uses that word? Sometimes a verse pushes the question of God's being more explicitly – what did Paul mean by 'divine nature' in Rom 1:20 or the word 'deity' in Col 2:9. We cannot call ourselves exegetes of Scripture if we show no interest in grasping the meaning and significance of these words. The text of Scripture itself leads us to these questions and to refuse to ask them is not to honour Scripture but to silence it.

Second, there are key moments where the actions of God are specifically tied to his nature. We might think of Exod 3:14, "I AM WHO I AM," Heb 6:13-18, "since there was no one greater for God to swear by, he swore by himself," or Mal 3:6, "I the LORD do not change." Space prevents us from analysing these verses in detail, but the Scriptures make it clear that the redemptive acts of God, the faithfulness to his promises and long-suffering patience with his people flow out from his nature. This should be no surprise. What is done reflects the nature of the one doing it.

But third and finally, to sideline questions of God's nature in favour of God's actions is to misunderstand the biblical presentation of those actions. The Bible presents the end, the goal, of God's redemptive purposes as the knowledge of God. "Now, this is eternal life, that they know you, the only true God, and Jesus Christ, whom you sent" prays Jesus in John 17:3. Habakkuk 2:14 promises that one day "the earth will be filled with knowledge of the glory of the Lord, as the waters cover the sea." To know God is the highest end of any creature. Of course, this knowledge is more than knowledge of God's essence and attributes, but we have very little reason to believe it is less than that. Of course, we cannot know now as we will know then, but to refuse to ponder, reflect, and meditate on what God *has* revealed about himself suggests that we do not understand his redemptive purposes as well as we might think.

## two. Does the Bible Teach Classical Theism?

If, then, we do think that the doctrine of God is a biblically-warranted topic, we still need to ask whether classical theism is what the Scriptures teach. Is God really an eternal being without body, passions and parts, unable to change? At first glance, "no" seems to be the obvious answer. Scripture is full of texts that speak of God changing, and responding emotionally. So how did the finest minds of the first seventeen centuries of the church, who read the very same biblical texts, arrive at the conclusion that, for instance, change is impossible for God?

The answer comes from understanding one of their foundational principles: God is Creator.

### a. God as Creator

The classical doctrine of God begins with the principle that all reality exists in one of two ways – created or uncreated. In Rev 4:11 the twenty-four elders sing,

> **Rev 4:11**
> *"You are worthy, our Lord and God,*
> *to receive glory and honour and power,*
> *for you created all things,*
> *and by your will they were created and have their being."*

In doing so, the elders are summarising a thread of teaching about God that runs through from the very first words of Gen 1:1, that there is a distinction between Creator and creature and only God dwells on the uncreated side of that divide. He is the one who gives being to all and, therefore, receives his being from no one else. He is, as the four living creatures never stop saying in Rev 4:9, "the Lord God Almighty, who was, and is, and is to come." He is thus worthy to receive glory, honour and power as the uncreated Creator.

It is from this distinction that all the affirmations of classical theism flow – that God is unchanging, eternal, etc. – for they are all ways of saying, from various angles, that God does not receive being from his creation but is always the giver; he is never made, he is always the maker. The absence of any other power or entity that conditions or affects God is expressed in his self-identification in Exod 3:14: "I AM WHO I AM." There is no limitation or restriction on the fullness of his life. He is, therefore, infinite, since nothing restricts him, and perfect, since nothing diminishes him. God's infinite perfection means that he never requires anything, in any way, from his creation; he is never subject to it but is always, infinitely and perfectly who he is and is thus able to give to creation limitlessly from his fulness.

Christian classical theism, therefore, insists that its major claims are all derived from the first phrase of the Apostles' Creed, "I believe in God the Father, Creator of heaven and earth." Yet, the question remains, if this is a necessary implication of the Bible, why are there so many texts that seem to flatly contradict it?

## b. Accommodation and Anthropomorphism

The answer is that the doctrine of creation not only has implications for our understanding of God's nature but also for how we read the Scriptures. Since we are created, dependent beings, limited by time and space, we can have no conception of what it is like to be uncreated, eternal, and independent. Therefore, for God to communicate to us, he must *accommodate* himself to our finite capacities. So the Scriptures speak of God having an arm or a throne or a face, to explain God's actions and character to us, without committing us to believe that God actually possesses a body or wears a robe. The technical term for this kind of language is *anthropomorphism*, God speaks, as it were, in a human form. We should not, however, restrict the concept of anthropomorphism simply to those occasions when the Scriptures speak of God in bodily terms. Our entire existence is conditioned by our creaturely limitations, and so God's revelation is, in Herman Bavinck's words, "anthropomorphic through and through." God reveals himself to us through the only means possible for creatures to know him: his creation. "In Scripture all heavenly things are portrayed to us in earthly shades and colours." So Bavinck explains,

I use the term here to also include what is more properly called *anthropopathism* which is where God describes himself with reference to human passions, not just human physical forms.

Herman Bavinck, *Reformed Dogmatics*, ed. John Bolt, trans. John Vriend, 4 vols. (Grand Rapids: Baker Academic, 2003), 2:99.

Bavinck, *Reformed Dogmatics*, 2:134.

*Although we can learn to know God's eternity only by and in time, his omnipresence by and in space, his infinity and immutability by and in the midst of finite and changeable creatures, yet these attributes do furnish us some – and even important – knowledge of God. Even though we cannot understand eternity in a positive sense, it means a lot to know that God is exalted above all the conditions of time. By means of that knowledge we, as it were, continually correct our notions concerning God. We speak of him in human terms and attribute to him a range of human qualities, but as we are doing this we are ever acutely conscious of the fact that all these properties pertain to God in a sense quite different from that in which we find them in creatures.*

Our knowledge of God is always conditioned by our creaturely limitations and God's revelation comes to us in a form most appropriate for those limitations. Even when God's revelation is at its fullest, in the incarnation of Jesus Christ, our knowledge of God does not escape our creaturely nature. Bavinck again:

*God himself comes to us through his whole creation and, in Christ's human nature, pitched his tent among us. This human nature, certainly, was not a fully adequate organ for his deity; in fact, his glory was even concealed by it. Still the fullness of the deity dwelt in Christ bodily: those who saw him saw the Father.*

Bavinck, *Reformed Dogmatics*, 2:107.

The fact that Christ's human nature did not fully reveal his deity does not mean that knowledge of God is impossible, however,

*It is not contradictory, therefore, to say that a knowledge that is inadequate, finite, and limited is at the same time true, pure, and sufficient. God reveals himself in his works, and according to that revelation we name him. He permits us to speak of him in language that is weak and human because he himself displayed his perfections to us in his creatures. Hence, in actual fact, it is not we who name God. Where would we get the ability and the right to do that? It is God himself who, through nature and Scripture, has put his splendid names in our mouth.*

ibid.

Whenever we read Scripture, therefore, we must take account of the fact that the one who is uncreated is revealing himself through created means and to created people. That he does so should never lead us to make the mistake that he himself is subject to the same limitations as the created order, even as he uses "earthly shades and colours" to reveal himself.

## c. Analogy

That God's revelation is accommodated to our creaturely capacities means that Scripture's revelation of God is always by way of analogy. Analogy is a much-misunderstood concept and often viewed with hostility because it appears to diminish the clarity and power of God's revelation of himself in Scripture. In reality, the reverse is the case. It is only because scriptural language is analogical that we can truly say that *God* is the one being revealed. How so? Analogy is based on the idea that Scripture's language about God always travels across the divide between Creator and creation, between infinite and finite. While there is a relationship between the way we understand a term and how it applies to God, there is never a strict identification between them.

A strict identification would be known as a *univocal* reading, which assumes that we can say something about the Creator *in the same sense* that we would say something of a creature.

Sometimes this is more obvious that at others. When Scripture calls God 'a rock' we instinctively know that a kind of comparison is being drawn. There is a relationship between God's steadfastness and the immobility of a rock, but it would be foolish to ask whether God is made of limestone or granite. The claim of those who say all our language about God is analogical is that this is true even when Scripture's speech about God seems more direct.

For instance, when John says that "God is love" (1 John 4:8) we might question whether he is speaking analogically. Surely here there is a direct correspondence between our love and God's love? Surely God's love is of the same species as our love? No. Even here, analogy is at play. Why? Because our experience of love, our knowledge of love, is only ever as finite, created beings. Even the highest expressions and experiences of our love are parcelled out over time, limited in their scope and extent. No human can give themselves exhaustively and infinitely in love in the way God can in eternity. Therefore, we have no direct experience of love which is eternal, infinite and uncreated due to our limitations of time, finitude and createdness.

What registers in our minds, therefore, when we read 'God is love' can only ever have an indirect relationship with, rather than exact correspondence to, the divine reality to which John refers. Does this mean that God has not revealed himself truly? No, because the love that we do know, limited and created as it is, is related to divine love, as an effect is related to its cause. Human love is a created effect of divine love and there is a connection between the two. Nevertheless, there is a difference between the eternal, infinite love of God and any love experienced by finite human beings.

There is, of course, a difference between saying 'God is a rock' and 'God is love.' The former is metaphorically true while the other is literally true. Love does exist in God's eternal life, but rocks do not; calling God a rock, therefore, is only true at the point of comparison, namely steadfastness, while God really is, wholly and fully, love. Yet, given the difference between created and uncreated, finite and infinite, the love we know is still only analogically related to the love of God in eternity. John Owen captures this beautifully in his *Communion with God*, where he describes the difference between our love and God's love,

Owen, *Works*, 2:29-30. Text slightly updated.

*They differ in this also: the love of God is like himself, equal, constant, not capable of augmentation or diminution; our love is like ourselves, unequal, increasing, waning, growing, declining. His, like the sun, [is] always the same in its light, though a cloud may sometimes interpose; ours, as the moon, has its enlargements and contractions.*

Affirming that all our language about God is analogical does not make God unknowable. Instead, it insists that the one who speaks in Scripture really is God. A God who could be described in language that directly corresponds to created realities would himself be limited to that creation. But with analogical language, the eternal, infinite, and perfect God has made himself known. Only if we understand God's revelation of himself as analogical can we really maintain that the infinite has spoken to the finite, that the Creator has spoken to the creature.

Analogy, accommodation, and anthropomorphism, therefore, are not a denial of divine revelation but its necessary ground, if the infinite God is to speak to finite creatures from eternity into time. Any doctrine of Scripture that dispenses with any, or all, of these concepts must implicitly deny either that God is infinite or that we are finite. That is to say, the alternative to recognising accommodation, anthropomorphism and analogy is either a God who exists within the created order or creatures that transcend it. Given the scriptural injunctions against idolatry (worshipping the finite) and human pride (denying our God-given limitations) we would be wise to steer clear of both.

## d. Reading Difficult Texts with Calvin

Recent scholarship has demonstrated that Calvin and his successors are not fundamentally at odds with each other. The most thorough demolition of the 'Calvin vs the Calvinists' thesis is found in Richard Muller's 'Calvin and the 'Calvinists': Assessing Continuities and Discontinuities between the Reformation and Orthodoxy' (parts 1 and 2) printed in his *After Calvin: Studies in the Development of a Theological Tradition* (Oxford: Oxford University Press, 2003).

How, then, do we interpret the texts that appear to show that God does change? Let us look at how one Scripture reader, John Calvin, handles some of those texts. Calvin is an appropriate choice because he is often viewed as someone who is committed to the text and as someone who stands apart from the rigid theological systems of later Calvinist or Reformed Theology. How, then, does Calvin deal with a verse like Gen 6:6, "The Lord regretted that he had made human beings on the earth, and his heart was deeply troubled"? Does he affirm, on the basis of the 'plain reading' of the text, that God does indeed change and can be grieved? He does not. Instead Calvin writes,

John Calvin, *Commentaries on the First Book of Moses Called Genesis*, commenting on Gen 6:6.

*The repentance which is here ascribed to God does not properly belong to him, but has reference to our understanding of him. For since we cannot comprehend him as he is, it is necessary that, for our sakes he should, in a certain sense, transform himself. That repentance cannot take place in God, easily appears from this single consideration that nothing happens which is by him unexpected or unforeseen. The same reasoning, and remark, applies to what follows, that God was affected with grief. Certainly God is not sorrowful or sad; but remains forever like himself in his celestial and happy repose: yet, because it could not otherwise be known how great is God's hatred and detestation of sin, therefore the Spirit accommodates himself to our capacity.*

Calvin begins with a clear affirmation of what we have just discussed, that neither repentance nor grief can properly be applied to God. Why? Because God is eternal, so "nothing happens which is by him unexpected or unforeseen", and impassible, and thus he "remains forever like himself in his celestial and happy repose." Calvin concludes that the apparently 'passible' language of these verses have "reference to our understanding of him" since the "Spirit accommodates himself to our capacity." But to what end? How can it help us to know God if the Bible ascribes repentance to one who cannot repent or grief to one who cannot grieve? Calvin answers that the words teach us that,

*ibid.*

*...from the time when man was so greatly corrupted, God would not reckon him among his creatures; as if he would say, 'This is not my workmanship; this is not that man who was formed in my image, and whom I had adorned with such excellent gifts: I do not deign now to acknowledge this degenerate and defiled creature as mine.' Similar to this is what he says, in the second place, concerning grief; that God was so offended by the atrocious wickedness of men, as if they had wounded his heart with mortal grief.*

So Gen 6:6 does teach us about God: sin is so contrary to his character that it elicits from him an act that if we saw it in a human would lead us to describe that person as grieved and repenting. As he explains in his *Institutes*,

Calvin, *Institutes*, I.17.13

*What, therefore, does the word 'repentance' mean? Surely its meaning is like that of all other modes of speaking that describe God to us in human terms... Now the mode of accommodation is for him to represent himself to us not as he is in himself, but as he seems to us. Although he is beyond all disturbance of mind, yet he testifies that he is angry towards sinners. Therefore, whenever we hear that God is angered, we ought not to imagine any emotion in him, but rather to consider that this expression has been taken from our own human experience; because God, whenever he is exercising judgment, exhibits the appearance of one kindled and angered.*

In the same section, and in a similar way, Calvin takes God's 'repentance' to mean a change in the way he acts towards us *from our perspective*:

*ibid.*

*Meanwhile neither God's plan nor his will is reversed, nor his volition altered; but what he had from eternity foreseen, approved and decreed, he pursues in uninterrupted tenor.*

Genesis 6:6 teaches us about God but, as Bavinck says, it does so, in "earthly shades and colours." Do we see in Calvin, then, someone who is embarrassed about the scriptural language of God's repentance and who uses his systematic framework to fit the text of Gen 6:6 into the procrustean bed of classical theism? No. Rather, we see Calvin reading Gen 6:6 in the light of the whole of Scripture, most notably the description of God as Creator in Gen 1, and seeking to understand the Scriptures as a coherent whole. Calvin's approach offers us a model for reading the Scriptures in the light of the Creator/creation distinction and its implications. Yet, in this regard at least, Calvin's approach is not unusual in the context of Christian history. Rather, it is the standard way that those who believe in the uncreated Creator, Father, Son and Spirit, have read and understood the Scriptures.

Procrustes is a figure from Greek mythology who would force houseguests to fit into an iron bed, either by stretching them on a rack, or by cutting off as much of their legs as necessary.

# three. Answering Objections

## a. Why Seek Coherence?

Many will feel uncomfortable with Calvin's approach. Does he not end up flattening the text with his own framework of what God is like? Many evangelicals will be impatient with concepts like 'anthropomorphism' or 'analogy' and instead insist that the text means what the text says! Here, though, we come across a curious feature of the way that contemporary British evangelicals engage with Scripture. Where we find two or more texts saying things that seem to be in tension historically, the evangelical instinct is, rightly, to seek for an explanation that brings the two into coherence. For instance, did Jesus clear the temple at the start of his ministry (John 2) or at the end (Matt 21), or how exactly did Judas die? This is virtually the ABC of evangelical biblical interpretation and apologetics and it springs from the correct assumption that as the word of God, the Scriptures must be free from contradiction.

When we turn to matters of theology, however, this desire for coherence is significantly reduced. We are urged not to 'impose a framework' on the text and simply let it speak for itself. This, though, is strange because the only reason to believe that the historical statements of Scripture are coherent is because the one who authors it is a coherent being. Our belief in the historical accuracy and coherence of Scripture rests, therefore, on a commitment about the nature of reality: that God is a God of truth and that, therefore, truth ultimately coheres. But if that is the case, surely we should expect his statements about himself to be coherent also?

It follows, then, that reading texts which speak of God regretting or changing his mind (e.g. Gen 6:6 or Hos 11:8) in the light of other texts like Rev 4:11 and Mal 3:6, is not to undermine Scripture's authority but flows directly from our belief in it. If Scripture was not the word of God, we would have no need to explain Gen 6:6 as teaching anything other than that God changed his mind in repentance. It is only because we believe that Gen 6:6 and Mal 3:6 and Rev 4:11 all come from the same authoritative source that we have grounds to pursue a conversation between them and expect that conversation to end in a harmonious whole.

Systematic theology, therefore, should never be understood to undermine the authority of Scripture; rather, to pursue a theological system is to testify that we believe Scripture's authority and the implications of that authority. We might put it like this: the classical doctrine of God should not be seen as a theological holiday from, or exception to, the evangelical doctrine of Scripture, for it is, in fact, its only true foundation.

### b. Shouldn't We Just Start with Jesus?

Some readers may have followed the preceding discussion with increasing impatience. Haven't we started in entirely the wrong place? Shouldn't a distinctively Christian doctrine of God begin, not with the notion of God as Creator, but with God as he reveals himself to us in Christ? And here, surely, is an insurmountable difficulty for the classical doctrine of God, for when we look at Christ we see one who hungers, thirsts, grows, suffers and dies and yet claims to reveal God unambiguously, to be one with the Father and, crucially, accepts his disciples' worship. If we accept his claims (and what use is evangelical theology if we do not?) then we have in Christ the revelation of a God who can change, a God who is open to new experiences and new relationships. Isn't the early church's understanding of God as immutable and impassible something that owes more to Greek philosophy than the revelation of God in Christ? A triumph of Aristotle over the Apostles?

The problem with this line of thinking is that it fails to appreciate the context in which Jesus claimed the rights of divinity, by accepting worship. There were plenty of human figures who claimed divine honours. The unique thing about the early church's worship of Jesus was not that they worshipped a man – the entire Roman Empire did something like that when it confessed Caesar as Lord – but the kind of God they thought Jesus was, namely the uncreated Creator of the Hebrew Scriptures. It was that Jesus claimed to be *this* God in human nature that was so radical and revolutionary. Maintaining the immutability and simplicity of Jesus' divinity was not, therefore, an unfortunate intrusion of the philosophy of Aristotle or Plato to an otherwise pristine Jewish faith but the aspect of Christianity most indebted to the revelation of the Old Testament. The early church teaching about the unchanging, absolute and infinite nature of Jesus' divinity owed little to Greek philosophy and everything to the very Hebrew conviction that to worship anything other than the uncreated Creator is idolatry.

It was to rescue Thomas from that charge of idolatry (and Jesus from the charge of blasphemy) that the early church maintained that when Thomas worshipped the risen Jesus in John 20:28, he was worshipping one who was divine, in full possession of the unchanging perfection of deity. Additionally, and somewhat paradoxically, only the notion that Jesus is fully God protects the integrity of Jesus' full humanity. It is only when we realise that Jesus' divine nature is *unable* to suffer, die or even change, that we realise that he experiences those things in his human nature, a human nature just like ours except for our sin.

The early church developed this account of Jesus' two natures by asking what the incarnate life of Christ reveals about God, and setting out their conclusions in the Chalcedonian Definition of A.D. 451. Put simply, that definition ascribes two natures to the single person of Christ: a divine nature which he has from eternity as the Second Person of the Trinity, and a human nature, which he assumes at the moment of conception in Mary's womb. Chalcedon seeks to do two things: first, to emphasise the unity of the natures since they belong to a single person, the Son; and second, to secure the distinction between the two natures which are recognised "without confusion, without change, without division, without separation; the distinction of natures being in no way annulled by the union." In this way, the Chalcedonian Definition allows us to ascribe change and suffering as genuinely real experiences of his human nature (and therefore of his person) while maintaining that Christ's divine nature remains unchangingly perfect and infinite.

## *four*. *The Implications of Classical Theism*

We have covered a lot of ground and done so relatively quickly. Perhaps, though, this discussion has felt like a long, slow, grim march of denials: "oh well, actually it doesn't mean that," "sorry, I'm afraid you can't say that", "actually that was in regard to his human nature so what you just said is probably heresy." Why keep trudging on, learning these unfamiliar and counter-intuitive concepts? Well, just as a man who learns a language for the sake of love must have his grammar corrected if he is ever to understand his beloved, so we should study the grammar of classical theism in order to better embrace the worship of the heavenly throneroom. For once we have become more familiar with the way biblical revelation works, we will find in classical theism not a dour, static God but one who is, in the words of Heinrich Bullinger, "the abundant fulness, that satisfies all men and all things: he is the everlasting well of all good things, which is never drawn dry." The affirmation that God is simple, unchanging, and perfect does not drain him of life but ensures that we ascribe him the maximum life possible, untouched by creaturely limitation or suffering. It is this God of infinite love, power, wisdom and goodness, who *is* love itself, who *is* goodness itself, who *is* life itself, who speaks to us in Scripture. It is this God of eternal perfection who steps into his creation in Christ. If we fail to see the God of classical theism in Scripture, we fail to see the most precious thing of which the Scriptures speak.

Heinrich Bullinger, *The Decades of Heinrich Bullinger: The First and Second Decades* (Cambridge: Cambridge University Press, 1849), 216.

What difference, then, does believing in and cherishing God as unchangingly, eternally perfect make? We can draw out just one implication of our discussion. If ultimate reality is found in the one who *is*, rather than in any historical process of becoming, then it re-orientates our assessment of human purpose. Of course, the eternal God is directing the process of salvation-history, but the goal of that process is the worship and praise of the eternal Father, Son and Spirit not only for his work in creation and redemption but simply for who he is.

This means that the final goal of human action is not achievement but worship; it is not usefulness but adoration. An approach to Scripture that concentrates on God's acts but not on his being, will always tend toward a task-orientated, activist Christianity where the urgent question is always, "are we advancing the Kingdom?" And we will almost always imagine that the Kingdom is advancing quicker in the church of 500 than in the church of 50 or through the gifted personal evangelist or Bible teaching rather than the stammering introvert. And, no doubt for the best of motives, the pull of pragmatism will always tug at our hearts and practice. Church services will be viewed as 'shop windows' for the visitors; any teaching regarded as peripheral to the gospel, ecclesiology, the sacraments, even the doctrine of the Trinity itself, can be side-lined if inconvenient; and the question will return, again and again, have I, or we, done enough? Exhaustion, burn-out, and breakdown cannot but be far behind.

But if we view the end of the Bible story, and therefore the purpose of human life, as worship of the Triune God, then we can bring the end into the middle of the story, here and now. Each Sunday, each church, no matter what size, can attain to the goal of human existence as they worship God in spirit and truth. The paraplegic, the housebound, the elderly can worship God with just as much piety as the bold Bible teacher or energetic evangelist and therefore bring just as much glory to God as they do so. Grasping the transcendent, unchanging, infinity of Father, Son and Spirit, swings the compass of hearts towards what is eternal rather than time-bound, what is infinite rather than finite. It liberates us from pragmatism and activism, because our first question becomes "did I worship God truly?" not "did I advance the kingdom?" Our value no longer arises from our gifts and achievements but from our status as adopted children of the infinite Father.

Such is the liberty and the joy available to those who discover the same God in the Scriptures as Augustine, Gregory, Calvin and innumerable other saints down the centuries. It may be, however, that the way we read the Scriptures will have to change in order to do so. We will have to relearn the grammar of analogy, accommodation and anthropomorphism again to truly grasp what God has revealed in his word. This may be a challenging and humbling process. Could it be that our very desire to take the word of God seriously has led us to downplay concepts, like accommodation and analogy, that those before us have understood as essential to understanding it correctly? Could our methods of interpreting the Bible actually obscure and minimise our vision of our Creator? If so, they do so at a great cost.

Anselm of Canterbury, the great 11th century theologian understood the knowledge and love of God as the supreme Triune Creator to be what Jesus tells us to ask for so that our "joy may be complete" (John 16:24). Of that knowledge he prayed,

*Anselm, Proslogion, chapter 26.*

> *Let my mind meditate on it, let my tongue speak of it, let my heart love it, let my mouth preach it. Let my soul hunger for it, let my flesh thirst for it, my whole being desire it, until I enter into the 'joy of the Lord (Matt 25:21), who is God, Three in One, 'blessed forever. Amen.' (Rom 1:25).*

May Anselm's prayer be answered in us all.

## Questions for further thought and discussion

1. Do you think we have emphasised what God has done for us at the expense of thinking about who God is? What do you make of Graham's suggestion that this produces a church culture in which we emphasise activity over the worship and adoration of God?

2. Graham has spoken about accommodation, anthropomorphisms, and analogy. Go back and check you understand what each of those mean and why Graham thinks they are worth learning.

3. One question the debate around the classical doctrine of God forces us to ask is the value we place on historical creeds such as the Apostles' Creed, the Chalcedon Definition, the Nicene-Constantinopolitan Creed, and so on. What status do these early confessions have in the life of your church or the training of your leaders? What status should they have, do you think?

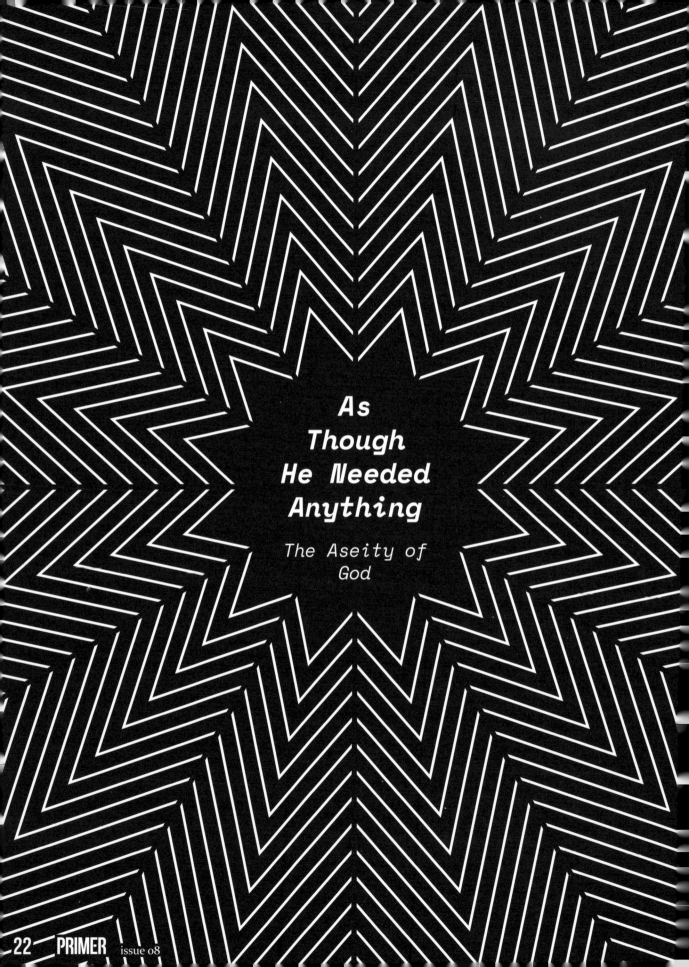

# As Though He Needed Anything

*The Aseity of God*

**GERALD BRAY** is Research Professor of Divinity at Beeson Divinity School, Samford University, Birmingham, Alabama and Director of Research for the Latimer Trust, London. He edited the journal *Churchman* from 1983 to 2018.

*"Who has ever given to God, that God should repay them?"*

*For from him and through him and for him are all things.*

*To him be the glory forever! Amen.*

*Romans 11:35-36*

When we speak about God with the term *aseity*, it is a way of joining in with Paul's "Amen." It is to confess that God is different from everything else; that all other beings are dependent on him for their existence; that only he stands alone and above everything else.

## Philosophical roots

Aseity is the belief that God has no origin outside himself and does not depend on anything else for his existence. It is a technical term adapted from the Latin *aseitas*, which was invented in the Middle Ages as a way of describing the absolute, independent being of God. The word is artificially constructed from *a se* ('from self').

The philosophical account of God's aseity can only be understood in light of the assumption that all beings are connected in a chain of cause and effect. Influenced by what they understood as Aristotelianism, Western European theologians of the twelfth and thirteenth centuries believed that God was the First Cause, or the Unmoved Mover of the universe, from whom everything else derived.

That is, the school of thought derived from the Ancient Greek philosopher Aristotle.

Whether a First Cause could really exist (without being the effect of some other cause) was a matter of debate. Several philosophers, then and since, have argued that such a view is untenable. In their opinion, the cause-effect model is ultimately circular (or self-contained) and cannot be thought of as deriving from a single, comprehensive source. If they are right, then aseity is a meaningless concept, since it cannot exist in reality. The Christian doctrine of aseity resolves this difficulty by putting the being of God outside the chain of cause and effect altogether.

## The Christian perspective

Christians do not believe in the aseity of God for purely philosophical reasons, even if they sometimes defend the principle along those lines. For us, aseity is a doctrine imposed by the revelation of God in Holy Scripture and made necessary by the fundamental distinction between the Creator and his creation. Everything in the created order has a cause, but that order is not self-generating. It was made out of nothing (*ex nihilo*) by God. It is not some extension or projection of his own being, but by an act of will he brought into existence something that is completely different from himself.

To understand God's aseity we must reject all attempts to connect God to the created order in a physical sense. The universe is not, and cannot be, part of his being, nor can anything in it be an extension of the divine nature. In this sense, God's aseity means that not only is his existence independent of the time and space-bound world, but also that nothing known to (or perceived by) us is adequate to describe him. Human attempts to discover God are doomed to fail for this reason – the finite cannot penetrate, let alone define, what is infinite.

Knowledge of God is possible, however, but only because he has revealed himself to us in specific terms that shed some light onto his being without being copied or derived from it. Human beings can (and do) have a personal relationship with their Creator, even though he is essentially different from them.

## Aseity in the Bible

Does the Bible teach a doctrine of divine aseity? In the most literal sense, it clearly does not. As we have already remarked, the word is an abstraction that was invented by theologians who were trying to express their faith in philosophical terms, something that the Bible almost never does. But if the term itself never appears in the Scriptures, the concept that lies behind it frequently does. It can be seen most clearly when a prophet or an apostle confronts the pagan polytheism of the surrounding world. When addressing the philosophers of Athens, for example, Paul expressed God's aseity when he said that "the Lord of heaven and earth does not live in temples made by man, nor is he served by human hands, as though he needed anything, since he himself gives to all mankind life and breath and everything."(Acts 17:24-25). Thus 'aseity' is a kind of shorthand, rather like the word 'Trinity,' that is used by theologians to refer to something that is revealed in the Bible and that is fundamental to our understanding of God.

First of all, the Scriptures clearly affirm the uniqueness of God – "I am the LORD, and beside me there is no other" (Isa 45:5). That assertion does not necessarily imply aseity, because it is theoretically possible to be a sovereign Lord without being uncaused, but in the case of God it points in that direction. If God had a cause, that cause would take priority over him and he would not be able to claim the absolute sovereignty that his revelation proclaims. Secondly, and in a similar vein, the Bible expresses the absolute being of God – "I AM WHO I AM" (Exod 3:14). Once again, this is not by itself proof of aseity, since it makes no mention of cause or effect, but it points in that direction and is fully compatible with it. The language of causation is used in the Bible of created things, but never of God, making it reasonable for us to assume that he is uncaused, even though that is not explicitly stated.

To find the doctrine of aseity in the Bible it is necessary to go beyond individual words and phrases and look at the broader context in which they are expressed. This is most clearly evident in the absolute distinction that the Bible makes between the Creator and his creation. No created thing can represent God – hence the prohibition of idolatry (Exod 20:4).

God's aseity is also evident in the fact that he has no need of sacrifices, even though he commanded his people to make them (Ps 40:6; 50:12-13). Sacrifice was for their benefit, not for his, because it taught people the seriousness of sin and reminded them of the great gulf that separated them from the Creator.

## Aseity in theological thought

Aseity can be expressed in a number of different ways. Karl Barth (1886-1968) spoke of God as being 'Wholly Other', or (in other words) completely different from us. Centuries before, the ancient theologian Origen (c.185-c.254) called the Christian God *autotheos* – God 'in himself.' God's divinity was not given to him by another, nor was it dependent on anything else. This is how God's aseity has traditionally been expressed. It is implied in the first article of both the Apostles' and the Nicene Creeds: "God the Father Almighty, Maker (or Creator) of heaven and earth," without being explicitly stated. As the Creator, God stands over and against everything else that exists – he is *autotheos*.

The aseity of God also relates to the Trinity in important ways. The three persons of the Trinity allow us to think of God subsisting eternally in a series of personal relationships. He does not require some other being for him to relate to. In other words, God does not need the creation in order to manifest his love; he can be fully loving in himself, because the persons of the Trinity love each other freely and completely. God has established relational connections with his creatures, but his love for them is an act of grace expressed outside himself and not an essential characteristic of his own being, which remains independent and completely different from anything that he has created. Thus the more we

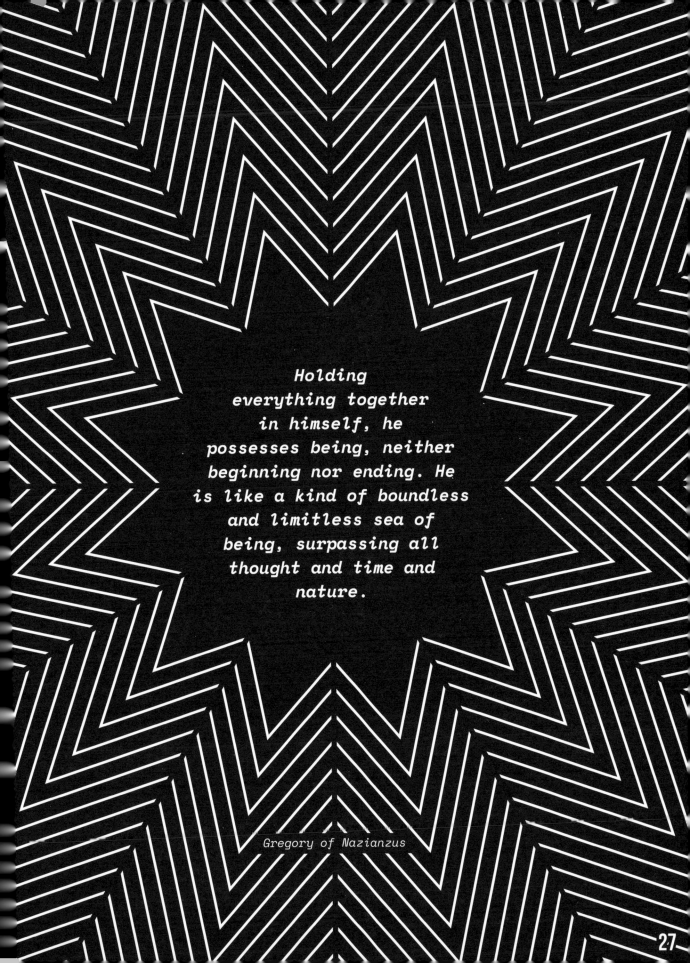

Holding everything together in himself, he possesses being, neither beginning nor ending. He is like a kind of boundless and limitless sea of being, surpassing all thought and time and nature.

Gregory of Nazianzus

appreciate God's aseity, the more we appreciate the wonder of his love, which reaches out beyond himself without being obliged to do so or needing to.

The aseity of God also means that he cannot be measured or judged by external criteria. For example, we cannot say that God is 'unjust' because he does not behave according to human notions of justice. We are told that we must not commit murder, but if God chooses to destroy people or things that is his prerogative as their Creator.

The Bible is quite clear that we are in no position to pass judgment on God, or to call him to account for things that lie beyond our understanding. He may choose to respond to our questions about his acts, but he is not obliged to do so, and his aseity is the main reason for that. He is not an integral part of the universe that he has made and is therefore not answerable to it for his actions. This freedom allows him to act according to his will, something that is not true of human beings. We often do what we do not want to do and feel constrained to behave in a certain way, but that is never true of God.

It is possible to think of God's freedom as allowing him to escape the obligations that he has voluntarily undertaken on our behalf, but that is to misunderstand it. God's freedom should be understood as a guarantee that he will fulfil his promises because he is able to do so. He will not turn to us on the day of judgment and say something like: "I would love to save you but cannot do so because of external constraints on my will that I am unable to escape." God's will can never be thwarted or suspended, because he is not beholden to any power outside himself. What he wills will come to pass, and if his will is our salvation, then nothing in heaven or on earth can separate us from the love of God (Rom 8:38-39).

## *Teaching God's aseity*

When communicating the principle of God's aseity to a congregation, the pastor should probably either avoid using the word itself, or else introduce it only after carefully preparing the ground in advance. The great Dutch theologian Herman Bavinck preferred to talk of God's 'independence', and his example is worth considering. It may be necessary to add other terms, like 'self-sufficiency' for example, in order to embrace the full range of meaning contained in the word aseity, but it is important to introduce the concept by using words that are already understood by one's hearers. Like it or not, aseity is an artificial term that is not in common use. The idea it is trying to express is important, but it needs to be mediated to a wider public by using words and examples that are meaningful to non-specialists.

The most fundamental of these examples is what Scripture says about the absolute distinction between the Creator and his creation. Creation has been made by God and is subject to laws of time and space that do not apply to the Creator.

A second way in which God's aseity is revealed is in his absolute sovereignty. God is the Lord of everything he has made and can dispose of it in any way that he chooses, without thereby affecting or diminishing his own being. This does not mean that God is arbitrary in what he decides to do, but that his will cannot be thwarted by powers or circumstances outside his control. God's complete freedom is revealed in his sovereignty and is the guarantee of his ability to act without any constraint or necessity.

Harder to grasp, but just as essential for our understanding of God's aseity, is that God is not constrained by his divine nature but is free to act. He is the uncreated One who is capable of creating; the eternal God who is capable of relating to time-bound creatures. Most remarkably, he is the immortal God who could experience death: God the Son became a man, took on sin and died for our salvation.

By speaking in this way and using the examples set out for us in Holy Scripture, the Christian instructor can convey the principles of divine aseity without becoming incomprehensible or detaching themselves from the understanding of their audience. A doctrine that at first sight seems alien to the faith and experience of many can thus be made accessible and be shown to be not only true in itself, but essential for a wider understanding of our faith and of our salvation in Christ.

## Questions for further thought and discussion

1. Theologian John Frame is really excited about the evangelistic potential of the truth of God's aseity: He writes that "it rebukes our pride and magnifies the power, wisdom, and grace of God." How has Gerald Bray's article helped you to see how it might do that?

   Check out his online article 'Divine Aseity and Apologetics'.

2. How is your own self-sufficiency a myth and an idol? How then does God's aseity become good news for proud or anxious or over-busy people?

# A SINGLE ENTIRE GOOD, AND THE ONLY GOOD

*Anselm and the Simplicity of God*

Anselm of Canterbury (1033-1109), although he was Italian, remains one of the most significant English theologians in the history of the church. Indeed, Anselm can be numbered as one of the theological 'A-Team' in the exalted company of its other members: Ambrose, Athanasius, Augustine and Aquinas. Much like the fictional 'A-Team', Anselm spent a lot of his life in exile and is best known for a crime he did not commit.

**NICK TUCKER** is a church minister in Birmingham, having formerly served with UCCF and then as a tutor at Oak Hill College. He is married to Sam and they have three kids. Nick has always enjoyed sport and is currently attempting to train for an Ironman Triathlon.

🐦 *@NJCTucker*

His alleged crime is that he invented the theory of penal substitution as a model of the atonement. This is doubly wrong. First, the doctrine of penal substitution is much older than Anselm and is firmly rooted in Scripture. Second, Anselm did not expound penal substitution. In his work *Cur Deus Homo* (Why did God become Man?) he offered an apologetic for the Incarnation and Atonement that is more accurately described as a *satisfaction* theory than an exposition of penal substitution.

A satisfaction theory thinks of Christ as repaying the debt of honour we owe to God, so that we are not punished, as opposed to penal substitution, in which Christ bears the punishment we deserve.

Anselm's fame, however, is much more justly based on his doctrine of God. His delightful short work, the *Proslogion* (in English: *A Discourse*), meditates on the wonder of God's being and wrestles with the apparent contradictions that he finds as he contemplates his Creator. He intended initially to call the work *Faith Seeking Understanding*. Like Augustine's *Confessions* the book takes the form of a prayer, and like the *Confessions* it has been influential well beyond the bounds of the church.

The reason for its fame is the apparently trivial argument Anselm presents for the necessary existence of God. Anselm defines God as "a being than which nothing greater can be conceived" and argues that therefore he must exist, for *being* is greater than *nonbeing*.

Anselm of Canterbury, *Proslogion*, ch 2. Translations are freely available on the internet.

This is what's known as the *ontological argument* for God's existence.

Christian and non-Christian thinkers have long chewed over that one. However, over the next few pages, our particular interest in the *Proslogion* is not so much about *whether* God exists, but about *how* he exists.

*Illustration depicting recreation of Anselm of Canterbury's seal.*

Anselm, *Proslogion*, ch 2.

Specifically, we shall consider the underlying (and rather overwhelming) view of God that forms the basis of Anselm's meditation. His view of God is that he is "a being than which nothing greater can be conceived" and so is, in the truest sense of the word, 'perfect.' Anselm recognises that this includes existence, but God's necessary existence implies that he lacks no property that would make him great: he is good in every way that it is possible to be good.

As we shall see, Anselm works out the implications of this with some care, by means of the idea of *simplicity*. He does so by considering a set of apparent contradictions in what we know of God and of goodness that have a very contemporary resonance, not least in the arena of virtue.

Mike Ovey used to help his students to grapple with some of the underlying issues that Anselm was addressing by quoting two very different thinkers from the twentieth century. The first was G. K. Chesterton, who lamented that:

Gilbert K. Chesterton, *Orthodoxy* (New York: John Lane Company, 1909), 53.

*The modern world is full of the old Christian virtues gone mad. The virtues have gone mad because they have been isolated from each other and are wandering alone. Thus some scientists care for truth; and their truth is pitiless. Thus some humanitarians only care for pity; and their pity (I am sorry to say) is often untruthful.*

*Commensurable* means that they do not map easily onto each other. I. Berlin 'Two Concepts of Liberty,' in *The Proper Study of Mankind*, ed. H. Hardy and R. Hausheer (London: Pimlico, 1998), 241.

Mike would then follow this up with a similar observation from Isaiah Berlin that "...human goals are many, not all of them commensurable, and in perpetual rivalry with one another." This situation is seriously destabilising for our wider culture, for it seems increasingly impossible to agree upon standards against which a life can be considered virtuous. The virtues have become so dislocated from each other that everyone has a radically different view of how to identify their heroes and villains. Take the feminist thinker Germaine Greer as an example. She was, for decades, a heroic figure amongst student radicals and a very hot ticket on the university speaking tour but has more recently faced calls for her 'no platforming' on university campuses.

The vision of virtue that we are offered in the *Proslogion* is profoundly different. God, who is the source of all goodness and all virtue, is a radically unitary being. He cannot be other than he is and so there is nothing true of him that he can lose and still be himself. This is the heart of the classical doctrine of simplicity. God is not a being who can be divided into parts.

Though Trinity, he is *one* and cannot be divided. Justice and mercy are not opposites or conflicting aspects of God's being, therefore; they are both expressions of his fundamental being. As Anselm will put it, "truly you are compassionate even *because* you are supremely just." So there is a unity and coherence to be found here. Unlike the ancient pagans, who were caught between competing deities, or our contemporaries struggling to choose between incompatible moral demands, the Christian can trust that God is free from even the hint of such discordance. This is what theologians mean when they talk about God's simplicity. It is not some abstract language game, it is an expression of confidence in the utter goodness of God in every respect.

Anselm, *Proslogion*, ch 10.

# THE PROSLOGION

*Anselm begins his discourse in **chapter 1** by invoking God's help. It is clear that he does not consider human reason alone as sufficient to investigate the being of God, who as creator is beyond both our investigation and comprehension due to our finitude and fallenness.*

Lord, if you are not here, where shall I seek you, being absent? But if you are everywhere, why do I not see you present? Truly you dwell in unapproachable light. But where is unapproachable light, or how shall I come to it? Or who shall lead me to that light and into it, that I may see you in it? Again, by what marks, under what form, shall I seek you?...

...Teach me to seek you, and reveal yourself to me, when I seek you, for I cannot seek you, except you teach me, nor find you, except you reveal yourself... Lord, I acknowledge and I thank you that you have created me in this your image, in order that I may be mindful of you, may conceive of you, and love you; but that image has been so consumed and wasted away by vices, and obscured by the smoke of wrong-doing, that it cannot achieve that for which it was made, except you renew it, and create it anew. I do not endeavour, O Lord, to penetrate your sublimity, for in no way do I compare my understanding with that; but I long to understand in some degree your truth, which my heart believes and loves. For I do not seek to understand that I may believe, but I believe in order to understand. For this also I believe, that unless I believed, I should not understand.

*This idea of "faith seeking understanding" shows the heart of Anselm's approach. He is not a philosopher thinking his way to God, he is a recipient of gracious revelation.*

*One of the key questions in the Proslogion is: 'What are we to make of the apparent contradictions that we see in God, such as his justice and mercy (compassion)?' In **chapter 9**, Anselm argues that God's justice is not in conflict with mercy, but both are an expression of God's ultimate goodness.*

But how do you spare the wicked, if you are all just and supremely just? For how, being all just and supremely just, do you do anything that is not just? Or, what justice is that to give him who merits eternal death everlasting life? How, then, gracious Lord, good to the righteous and the wicked, can you save the wicked, if this is not just, and you do not do anything that is not just? Or, since your goodness is incomprehensible, is this hidden in the unapproachable light wherein you dwell? Truly, in the deepest and most secret parts of your goodness is hidden the fountain whence the stream of your compassion flows.

For you are all just and supremely just, yet you are kind even to the wicked, even because you are all supremely good. For you would be less good if you were not kind to any wicked being. For, he who is good, both to the righteous and the wicked, is better than he who is good to the wicked alone; and he who is good to the wicked, both by punishing and sparing them, is better than he who is good by punishing them alone. Therefore, you are compassionate, because you are all supremely good. And, although we can see why you do reward the good with goods and the evil with evils; yet this, at least, is most wonderful, why you, the all and supremely just, who lacks nothing, bestows goods on the wicked and on those who are guilty toward you.

*Anselm refuses to fall into the kind of unbelief Hilary of Poitiers describes, which "takes such wisdom as its own finite perception can attain, and, measuring infinity by that petty scale, concludes that what it cannot understand must be impossible" (On the Trinity, Book 3). But nor does he counsel despair by denying that God can ever be truly known. For Anselm, God can truly be known, as he reveals himself to his people, but remains greater than we can imagine and beyond our finding out.*

The depth of your goodness, O God! The source of your compassion appears, and yet is not clearly seen! We see whence the river flows, but the spring whence it arises is not seen. For, it is from the abundance of your goodness that you are good to those who sin against you; and in the depth of your goodness is hidden the reason for this kindness...

...For, though it is hard to understand how your compassion is not inconsistent with your justice; yet we must believe that it does not oppose justice at all, because it flows from goodness, which is no goodness without justice; nay, that it is in true harmony with justice. For, if you are compassionate only because you are supremely good, and supremely good only because you are supremely just, truly you are compassionate even because you are supremely just. Help me, just and compassionate God, whose light I seek; help me to understand what I say.

*A real danger for the theologian can be a sense of "mastery" over God: after all we talk about mastering a subject. Anselm on the other hand is self-consciously mastered by his subject.*

It is also just that you should punish the wicked. For what is more just than that the good should receive goods, and the evil, evils? How, then, is it just that you should punish the wicked, and, at the same time, spare the wicked? Or, in one way, do you justly punish, and, in another, justly spare them? For, when you punish the wicked, it is just, because it is consistent with their deserts; and when, on the other hand, you spare the wicked, it is just, not because it is compatible with their deserts, but because it is compatible with your goodness.

*Here Anselm begins to develop his answer. Although God acts to judge some and spare others, he does not do so because he is inconsistent. In fact, his mercy is an expression of his justice.*

For, in sparing the wicked, you are as just, according to your nature, but not according to ours, as you are compassionate, according to our nature, and not according to yours; seeing that, as in saving us, whom it would be just for you to destroy, you are compassionate, not because you feel an affection (affectum), but because we feel the effect (effectum); so you are just, not because you repay us as we deserve, but because you do that which becomes you as the supremely good Being. In this way, therefore, without contradiction you do justly punish and justly spare...

*Anselm's point here is that God does not contradict the justice of his nature in sparing us. To demonstrate this he argues, (using a light pun: affectum/effectum) that God is not moved out of his disposition to justice by an external force that acts on his emotions (an affectum) but that his expression of his innate goodness in sparing the wicked is experienced (in effectum) by us as compassion. In other words, although different people experience God's actions differently, this should not be taken to imply that God has 'mood swings' which alternate between a predisposition towards justice and a willingness to forgive.*

Truly, then, all the paths of the Lord are mercy and truth (Ps 25:10); and yet the Lord is righteous in all his ways (Ps 145:17). And assuredly without inconsistency: For, it is not just that those whom you do will to punish should be saved, and that those whom you do will to spare should be condemned. For that alone is just which you do will; and that alone unjust which you do not will. So, then, your compassion is born of your justice.

*Anselm's argument for simplicity is the same as that which Calvin deployed half a millennium later in his Institutes: although we talk about God by treating his 'attributes' as though they were distinct, this is simply because we do not have the capacity to perceive the fulness of God in one go. This is how Anselm puts it in **chapter 18**:*

Assuredly you are life, you are wisdom, you are truth, you are goodness, you are blessedness, you are eternity, and you are every true good. Many are these attributes: my straitened understanding cannot see so many at one view, that it may be gladdened by all at once. How, then, O Lord, are you all these things? Are they parts of you, or is each one of these rather the whole, which you are? For, whatever is composed of parts is not altogether one, but is: in some sort plural, and diverse from itself; and either in fact or in concept is capable of dissolution. But these things are alien to you, than whom nothing better can be conceived of. Hence, there are no parts in you, Lord, nor are you more than one. But you are so truly one and the same with yourself, that in no respect are you unlike yourself; rather you are unity itself, indivisible by any conception. Therefore, life and wisdom and the rest are not parts of you, but all are one; and each of these is the whole, which you are, and which all the rest are.

*This is such a helpful corrective to contemporary views of God that appear to put his love and justice at odds with each other. As appealing as it might seem at first glance, to suggest that in such a context "love wins", the cost of such a construction is that it leaves us with a God to whom goodness and justice are optional extras.*

*Finally, in **chapter 23**, Anselm starts to relate simplicity to the Trinity. This is another place where simplicity is important. We have already seen how it stops us playing different attributes off against one another. Now Anselm shows how this emphasis on God being 'without parts' stops us thinking of the Father, Son and Spirit as the three parts that make up God. Each person of the Trinity is distinct, but not a division of God.*

*Anselm presents an approach to understanding the Trinity here that comes straight from Augustine, particularly the emphasis on the Spirit as the bond of love between Father and Son. The great strength of his approach is that it upholds the distinction between the persons without dividing God up into parts. This avoids the ancient heresies of Sabellianism (denying that God is eternally three persons) and Tritheism (arguing that the three persons are three gods). The emphasis on love underlines the reality of personhood. God may be simple and without parts, but he is relational and loving at the very core of his being.*

...This good you are, you, God the Father; this is your Word, that is, your Son. For nothing, other than what you are, or greater or less than you, can be in the Word by which you do express yourself; for the Word is true, as you are truthful. And, hence, it is truth itself, just as you are; no other truth than you; and you are of so simple a nature, that of you nothing can be born other than what you are. This very good is the one love common to you and to your Son, that is, the Holy Spirit proceeding from both. For this love is not unequal to you or to your Son; seeing that you do love yourself and him, and he, you and himself, to the whole extent of your being and his. Nor is there anything else proceeding from you and from him, which is not unequal to you and to him. Nor can anything proceed from the supreme simplicity, other than what this, from which it proceeds, is.

But what each is, separately, this is all the Trinity at once, Father, Son, and Holy Spirit; seeing that each separately is none other than the supremely simple unity, and the supremely unitary simplicity which can neither be multiplied nor varied. Moreover, there is a single necessary Being. Now, this is that single, necessary Being, in which is every good; nay, which is every good, and a single entire good, and the only good.

*To Anselm, God, in his simple perfection, is the one and only source of joy and fulfilment. The* Proslogion *is not a matter of merely academic or intellectual enquiry, it is an act of worship and an expression of the author's quest for holy joy:*

I pray, O God, to know you, to love you, that I may rejoice in you. And if I cannot attain to full joy in this life may I at least advance from day to day, until that joy shall come to the full. Let the knowledge of you advance in me here, and there be made full. Let the love of you increase, and there let it be full, that here my joy may be great in hope, and there full in truth. Lord, through your Son you do command, nay, you do counsel us to ask; and you do promise that we shall receive, that our joy may be full. I ask, O Lord, as you do counsel through our wonderful Counsellor. I will receive what you do promise by virtue of your truth, that my joy may be full. Faithful God, I ask. I will receive, that my joy may be full. Meanwhile, let my mind meditate upon it; let my tongue speak of it. Let my heart love it; let my mouth talk of it. Let my soul hunger for it; let my flesh thirst for it; let my whole being desire it, until I enter into your joy, O Lord, who are the Three and the One God, blessed for ever and ever.

**AMEN**

## Questions for further thought and discussion

1. Where does our culture feel torn by competing values and rivalries? What is the fruit of that in people's lives?

2. Why is Anselm so concerned to emphasise that God is not "composed of parts"?

3. Anselm wonderfully captures the way in which thinking about God is not a philosophical task which we are capable of as rational beings. And yet he doesn't despair. Why not? How does he model to us how to pray and how to think?

GOD
FUL
VOL

# The Doctrine of Divine Impassibility

**CHRISTOPHER STEAD** is the Mike Ovey Fellow at Oak Hill College. He used to practise as a chancery barrister, before training at Oak Hill and then completing a curacy in London. Alongside teaching doctrine, he is undertaking PhD studies through the University of Aberdeen in the field of Christology.

*@steadyc1986*

*"At the cost of the dizzying highs of human emotion, we have suppressed its abysmal lows."*

Thus says the villain in one of my favourite films, the 2002 dystopian sci-fi thriller, *Equilibrium*. Christian Bale stars as a cleric of the Tetragrammaton regime. Their aim is to eliminate all forms of emotion and creative expression in order to eradicate the causes of human conflict. One of the regime's key weapons in the fight is the drug *prozium*, which suppresses all human affection. Yes, feelings such as love, joy, and the appreciation of beauty, are destroyed, but the tyrants believe this is justified because it removes the threat of fickle and dangerous moods.

In light of that nightmare-ish vision, what should we make of the fact that for nearly two millenia, the church has insisted that God is "without... passions"? You can understand why people have begun asking whether we have been guilty of administering a dose of prozium to God himself.

This is the Protestant way of putting it. See e.g. Article 1 of the *39 Articles of Religion*, Chapter 2 of the *Westminster Confession of Faith*, *Savoy Declaration*, and *2nd London Baptist Confession of Faith*.

This idea that God is "without passions" – otherwise known as *divine impassibility* – has traditionally meant that God cannot suffer or undergo emotional change. Thomas Weinandy, a widely-respected Catholic theologian, defines it like this:

*Impassibility is that divine attribute whereby God is said not to experience inner emotional changes of state whether enacted freely from within or effected by his relationship to and interaction with human beings and the created order.*

This comes from the *New Catholic Encyclopedia*. Available online by searching *encyclopedia.com*.

At first glance, then, the charge of theological prozium seems to stick. For Christians committed to the radical and other-worldly love of the God who takes us for his children (1 John 3:1-3), it seems counter-intuitive to assert that he does not undergo emotional change, and I am aware of the challenge I face in seeking to defend it as a good thing. Nevertheless, the apostle in 1 John 3:1 is struck by the *otherness* of God's love – it is not a usual kind of love at all. And I'm going to try and persuade you that divine impassibility is part of that tapestry of interconnected attributes that preserve the truth that God is not usual; he is not just a bigger version of us. Divine impassibility tries to answer this question: what kind of God is free enough to lavish such a love upon sinners that he not only treats them as friends, he makes them his *children*? The doctrine brings conceptual coherence to the consistent biblical testimony to God's perfect and infinite love that relentlessly reaches through all hostility and suffering and grabs hold of rebels to bring them home.

Literally, he exclaims "Behold, *from what place is this love?*"

# HISTORY

Over the last century or so, divine impassibility has been rejected or heavily qualified by many writers, at both the academic and more popular levels. In part this is because, in the face of suffering, people want to appeal to a God who also suffers. It also reflects a suspicion of systematic theology and a nervousness that Greek philosophy has unduly influenced our doctrine.

Of course, the way to settle the question is to search the Scriptures, and we will go there soon. But please note: if we come to the conclusion that

Scripture does not teach divine impassibility in the traditional sense, we have made a significant departure from the vast witness of most of the church in nearly all of its history.

In truth, divine impassibility is one of the most stable theological positions that the church has known. As E.L. Mascall notes,

*There are few doctrines that can claim in their support so long and consistent a witness in the tradition of Christian theology as the doctrine of the impassibility of God.*

E.L. Mascall, *Existence and Analogy* (London: Longmans, 1949), 134.

It was simply assumed on all sides in the creedal debates of the fourth and fifth centuries. It can be found in writers as early as Ignatius (who died around A.D. 110); it is deployed without discomfort by all of the best-known church fathers; and at the end of the eighth century, John of Damascus can list it alongside other attributes without comment or defence.

Paul Gavrilyuk's survey of impassibility and Christology in the first eight centuries of Christian theology stresses a very important point: to use some rather technical language, divine impassibility was an "apophatic qualifier". Namely, Christian pastors and theologians appealed to impassibility to insist that God does possess things like love, joy, and delight, in himself, but that he does so in ways that are *not* like us. To say that God does not suffer, or experience emotional change, was not intended by these writers to say that God is like a lifeless rock; rather, it meant that "emotionally-coloured characteristics" that God definitely possesses must exist in him in a way that is fitting for the infinite and unimprovable God.

Gavrilyuk is also helpful in answering the common charge of *Hellenisation* laid against the classical attributes of God. After examining the complex variety of Greek philosophical schools on this issue, he concludes that the early church could not have been agreeing with pagan positions "simply because the philosophers did not agree among themselves." Even when the early Christians used common philosophical concepts, they submitted to the Bible when explaining them. Most fundamentally, the concept of God as uncreated Creator in contrast to creation was

Apophatic theology is, put in the strongest terms, the way of speaking about God that only says things that God cannot be; that, in light of his 'otherness' as the uncreated Creator of all, infinite and beyond our comprehension, we do not 'know' anything positive about him. Now, a totally apophatic (or 'negative') theology seems a bit extreme, particularly because in saying we are ignorant about something necessarily means we do know something about it, namely that we cannot know it! But there is great value in including 'negative' theology in our thinking about God, not least because it helps us remember to avoid idolatry and making God in our image.

Paul Gavrilyuk, *The Suffering of the Impassible God: The Dialectics of Patristic Thought* (Oxford: OUP, 2004), 16, 51. Recently, Reformed theologian Paul Helm, who is a passionate advocate of divine impassibility, has proposed a word to capture this truth – 'themotion.' He wants to capture both that God does not have emotions like us, but also that God in himself does have true love, and happiness, in ways that we cannot possibly comprehend. See Paul Helm, "The Impossibility of Divine Passibility," in *The Power and Weakness of God: Impassibility and Orthodoxy* (ed. Nigel M. de S. Cameron; Edinburgh: Rutherford, 1990).

That is, to become more Greek. In this context, to use Greek philosophical ideas and distort the biblical faith.

Gavrilyuk, *Suffering*, 36.

See, e.g., Weinandy, *Does God Suffer?* 70-74; Gerald Bray, *The Doctrine of God* (Leicester: IVP, 1993), 58.

For example, on divine 'repentance': "Though he is incapable of every feeling of perturbation, [God] declares that he is angry with the wicked. Wherefore, as when we hear that God is angry, we ought not to imagine that there is any emotion in him, but ought rather to consider the mode of speech accommodated to our sense." John Calvin, *Institutes of the Christian Religion* (Peabody, Mass.: Hendrickson Publishers, 2008), I.xvii.3. See also II.xiv.2.

Samuel Renihan, *God Without Passions: A Reader* (Palmdale, CA.: RBAP, 2015). Renihan's *Reader* records some Reformed writers who employed a distinction between *passions* and *affections* to say that things we experience as emotions might be present in God, but not like in us (and definitely without change!). For many, both terms were unhelpful to use of God, and were denied altogether.

John Owen, *Vindicae Evangelicae* in *The Works of John Owen (Vol. 12)* (ed. William Gould; London: Banner of Truth, 1966), 108-9.

distinctively Christian, and non-negotiable, and this shaped the way the doctrine developed.

Throughout the Middle Ages, theologians continued to affirm and restate this doctrine, and the Reformers inherited it without much trouble at all. Calvin, for instance, didn't much discuss traditional divine attributes in the *Institutes* (although they receive attention throughout his commentaries), and where they are mentioned, they are usually accepted. And Samuel Renihan has collected statements of Reformed and evangelical writers from the Reformation to the beginning of the 18th century which demonstrate consistency of belief in divine impassibility.

If history shows the consistent approval of divine impassibility, it also provides examples of the way it sustains healthy devotional lives. John Owen, for example, would strenuously deny affections and passions in God because they only properly belong to finite creatures:

> ...to ascribe affections properly to God is to make him weak, imperfect, dependent, changeable, and impotent.

God's infinite blessedness cannot be bettered or altered by creation. And yet, Owen is a man of immense prayer who enthused about communion with this God. For him, the impassibility of God was not an obstacle to knowing the joyous love of God but its underpinning.

The very identity and nature of God was not a minor issue for now-departed saints. To be gospel-people we must be attentive to the gospel's God. Our evangelical heritage, then, is that God is 'without passions', being unaffected by things outside of him and without the possibility of emotional change within.

# THE BIBLICAL WITNESS

## Preliminary Issues

How might we show that impassibility emerges from Scripture? *The Westminster Confession of Faith* (*WCF*), which provides proof-texts for doctrinal statements, supplies Acts 14:15 for "without... passions." Paul and

Barnabas dissuade the people of Lystra worshipping them as gods, and Paul announces "We also are men, of like nature with you" (ESV). The phrase 'of like nature' translates *homoiopatheis*, which could be translated 'of like passions'. So, it could be argued, Paul is showing that passions are that which distinguish humans from gods.

However, instead of offering a proof-text, it is better to proceed another way. Earlier in this issue, Graham Shearer has helpfully set out some principles which necessarily arise from evangelical convictions concerning the unity of the Bible as the infallible word of the one God. As well as letting Scripture interpret Scripture, we must also apply the principle of "good and necessary consequence" when reading the Bible. Every text has the entire Bible as its context, so we ask the question, "what must be true about God if every word of Scripture is taken seriously?"

*WCF, 1.6.*

I will argue that impassibility is the necessary inference to draw about the God who does all the Bible says he does, and is all the Bible says he is. As Mike Ovey taught his students, impassibility reflects one aspect of what God must be like to keep his promises.

## *The Glorious Creator*

We begin with the biblical story, and we first encounter God as the *Creator* of all that is. God does not stand within the order of life and being as we know it. Rather, he "created all things", giving and sustaining their being by his will, a reality which calls forth all honour and glory to be rendered to him alone (Rev 4:11). Unlike the idols, who are made by humans and depend on them for their existence (Isa 44), God is the incomparable one who "brings out the starry host one by one and calls forth each of them by name. Because of his great power and mighty strength, not one of them is missing" (Isa 40:25-26).

God is not merely like us but bigger; he is the uncreated Creator of all, who has in his being all that is necessary to give life and breath and everything to humanity, and by extension, to the entire universe (Acts 17:24). There is a fundamental *otherness* to his existence; as one theologian once said, we don't rightly talk about God by saying "MAN!" in a loud voice. His ways and thoughts are not like ours (Isa 55:8-9). As the great 'I AM', whose name indicates the pure and infinite existence that he is (Exod 3:14) and whose very being can only be known through kind condescension (Exod 33:12-23), God is not an agent within the universe, subject to the same terms and conditions.

For instance, God is eternal. He is without beginning and end, and has no *succession* either. That is, he does not experience one thing after another. He is without time, because he created time itself. In the creation narrative, God creates the markers of time, and the 'beginning' is an absolute beginning. In Psalm 90, God can look upon a thousand years and see that

See Gordon Wenham, *Genesis: 1-15* (WBC; Nashville: Thomas Nelson, 1987), 14, who draws this conclusion.

period as though in a single glance. In Psalm 102:26-27, the Creator God is contrasted with the succession and decay of the very heavens and earth. He is not limited by anything in the universe, and gazes upon it, in all dimensions and temporal extensions, with one view, knowing "the end from the beginning" (Isa 46:9-10).

Being without succession, then, means that God does not *change*. This is precisely because he is *not* like us, in whom change and becoming are necessary characteristics (Num 23:19; cf. Mal 3:6; Jas 1:17). He is the sovereign one, outside the influence and limit of the world. "He sits enthroned above the circle of the earth, and its people are like grasshoppers" (Isa 40:22). He is infinitely alive with a life that is from himself, and out of which he has infinite resources to create and sustain the life of others (Isa 40:12-31; cf. Ps 36:9; John 5:26). He does all that he pleases, working out all things according to his will as he blesses his chosen people with eternal love and glory in adoption, and with a place in a world where pain and tears are no more (Ps 115:3; Eph 1:3-14; John 17; Rev 21-22).

## The Perfect, Triune God

God is *perfect*. He is that than which no greater can be conceived (and can therefore only swear by himself: Heb 6:13). As the ultimately perfect and unimprovable being, he is the inexhaustible fountain of life for all that is, the transcendent source and ground of all goods in the created universe. He is the sole reason for his own life and perfection. That is, all the goods, and life, that are *in* God, must be identical *with* God, otherwise he would depend on something outside himself, or prior to himself, in order *to be who he is*.

See the extract from Anselm in this edition of *Primer*.

This belief, that God is not made up of anything else but himself, is the belief that God is *simple*. He alone gets all the glory for being himself, and there is nothing in him that is not identical with him. He himself *is* infinite life, and love, and blessedness. Therefore, theologians have said of God that he is *pure act*. That is, he cannot be moved to a greater state of perfection, or have his perfect life undermined, because he simply is who he is, maximally engaged. As Mike Ovey used to say: "God is at full volume, all the time."

See the article by Gerald Bray in this edition of *Primer*.

God's perfection, and his existence as Trinity, are closely linked. In his eternal relations, in which the Father gives all that he is and has to the Son (except being Father) and the Holy Spirit proceeds from them both, God is utterly full and happy. He cannot be made better by anything outside himself, and is gloriously safe in this blessedness. This is his *aseity* – his independence *from* the world because his life is absolutely full in himself (Acts 17:24-26; cf. Ps 50:8-12; Job 41:11). His one being, identical with these relations, is therefore full of movement and life and limitless love, so he cannot suffer any lack, nor be improved. Creation and salvation were not acts God needed to do; he freely chose to *give*, and this generosity is free precisely because God gains nothing from it.

# DRAWING THE STRANDS TOGETHER

We can start drawing things together for impassibility. God's existence as the uncreated Creator means that the suffering and change within this fallen world are not part of his own plane of existence. He sustains all things immediately and intimately, not as part of this universe but transcending it at every point.

We only have so much room in our lives for other people, and, as finite creatures, when we relate to them, it has an effect upon us. When someone new comes into my life, something's got to give, in terms of effort, attention, time, and the like. I am changed because of the new relationship. But God is not like us. He is infinite. He does not need to make room for us, because as the very source of our existence he is infinitely capable of relationship. Nothing's got to give in God. Nothing from our existence overflows into his, because our lives are not the same as his.

Furthermore, all that is in God – his will, his intellect, his 'affections' – are identical with who he is, and therefore cannot change, just as he cannot change. However, God's unchangingness (or *immutability*) is not because he is inert and disinterested, but because he couldn't be *more* alive and loving. If his emotions could undergo change, then there would be something in God which had potential to improve. He would have a lack, an imperfection.

His delight in himself as the triune God is eternal, and creation does not weary him or, put most strongly, make a difference to him. But this is not a bad thing! Precisely because God is such, and cannot be subject to the influence of anything outside himself, he is free to lavish love upon us without a hint of selfishness or compulsion for gain; indeed, his impassibility is "the absolutely inextinguishable vehemence of infinite love."

David Bentley Hart, 'No Shadow of Turning: On Divine Impassibility' in *Pro Ecclesia* XI, 2 (2002), 197.

Impassibility does not deny joy, delight, and love in God. It attributes those things to God without the limitations and imperfections that attach to them when present in us. God's perfect, generous, and steadfast love for his people is not eradicated by impassibility, but established by it.

What then do we make of those instances in Scripture where humanity seems to experience different emotions and dispositions of God? Traditionally, it is suggested that this is because God's *affections* are the way in which he wills himself to be known at varying points in time and space. In himself, God remains unchanging, but as we change, we experience that unchanging God in different ways. His affections are therefore our experience of the effects he wills us to experience; his simple essence is experienced in finite ways that look like human emotions *as if* God were under conditions of embodiment, time, and space. This is simply the recognition of the two standpoints that follow from the biblical Creator-creature distinction. God's thoughts, and perspective, are not like ours (Isa 55:8-9; Deut 29:29), and therefore what he reveals is never going to exhaust all that is true of him in that moment. He uses language that we recognise from our relationships with other creatures, so that we can learn something about ourselves and how our actions affect our relationship to God; but because he is not like us, it doesn't mean the same thing for him. It doesn't make it any less *true*, but we need to remember that it is revealed for our capacities, not as a one-to-one correspondence to God's infinite being.

Psalm 136 helpfully illustrates this principle. In this song, the repeated refrain is that God's "steadfast love endures forever." There is one characteristic of God (his steadfast covenant love), and yet this is experienced by different people in different ways, depending on where they stand in relationship to God. So, for Israel, God's steadfast love means salvation; for the Amorites and Bashanites, God's steadfast love means slaughter. God's wrath, then, is the expression of God's infinite love as experienced by those who put themselves outside it, in rebellion; they face that perfect love as judgment, as the love finds itself in the context of unredeemed evil.

In our own lives we can experience something similar. Arising out of the infinite love within his triune being, God sets his love on his people as he sees them in his Son. Remember, the love with which the Father loves the Son is freely put upon and within believers (John 17:26). So, even though we may have different experiences of our Father's love, as 'chiding' one moment, and 'smiling' the next, in different "dispensations of his grace", nevertheless the love itself which is fixed upon us and which is promised to us in eternity is nothing else than the infinite and unimprovable love that is identical with God's own being.

See John Owen, *Of Communion with God the Father, the Son, and the Holy Ghost*, in *Works: Volume 2* (ed. William Goold; London: Banner of Truth, 1966), 29-31, 31.

We finish our brief biblical case for divine impassibility with a return to the promises. In God's gospel promise, no possibility exists that he will not show himself to be the eternal resting place, and Father for those who are united to the Son by the Spirit. No intrusion of suffering will cloud his purpose, no emotional experience will affect his resolve, and he is not moved by the vagaries of feeling that would render his grace even slightly provisional. His promises are as unyielding as his being, and that means we can come to God in repentance, confident of forgiveness.

# OVERCOMING SOME OBJECTIONS

## Aren't we still ignoring the plain meaning of the Bible?

Still, there are those for whom the biblical depictions of divine emotion are too stubborn to be explained in the traditional manner. God is said to grieve (Gen 6:6; cf. Eph 4:30), to be afflicted (Isa 63:19), to relent of judgment in the face of human repentance (Jonah 3:10), to alter his plans in the face of prayer and bring healing (Isa 38:1-5), to have an anger that can be aroused by rebellion (Num 11:1), to experience deep yearning and moving compassion for his wayward people (Jer 31:20), and so on. God's *immanence* in the biblical story is seen as evidence that the old account of absolute *transcendence* must be wrong.

Immanence: God's involvement with and nearness to the world.

Transcendence: God's independence and distinction from the world.

The traditional reading of these texts sees them as descriptions of God in the language of human emotion to teach us something true rather than exhaustively reveal what God is actually like in himself. This is met with impatience amongst some, who regard this as the strait-jacketing of the Bible into an alien system.

These are known as *anthropopathisms* (anthropo=human; pathos=emotion/ suffering). They are related to *anthropomorphisms* (anthropo=human; morophs=form) which speak of God as if he had a human body.

Let's begin with the critique that God's immanence must make us careful about exaggeration of his transcendence. Following the example of Weinandy, we might want to ask the question: why put these two things in opposition? God's immanence is not a parallel mode of existence alongside his transcendence, or something that he does *in spite* of his transcendence. Rather, when God acts in and through history to save his people and draw them close into covenantal intimacy, he is revealing the very transcendence that allows him to act in this way. What kind of God can be immanent to Israel as her Creator, Covenant Lord, and Saviour? What kind of God can be as close and present as the God of Psalm 139? Only the God who is the uncreated Creator of all that is, and exists outside the limits of creation itself: "The words and actions by which and in which Yahweh revealed his presence are the very same words by which and in which Yahweh revealed his wholly and complete otherness."

Weinandy, *Does God Suffer?*, 53.

What about the idea that reading the relevant biblical passages as anthropopathisms allows theology to ride roughshod over exegesis? Well, for a start, no one comes to the Bible and simply 'reads it' without a load of presuppositions and assumptions. We all have an interpretive grid. As a crude example, I'd hope that any Christian would come to the Bible assuming that God exists, and that any interpretive option which permits the non-existence of God is not really an option. So, it may seem apparent to us that 'emotional' language attributed to God must mean for him what it would for us, but this is in itself an assumption. Or what about those biblical texts that tell us God has eyes, ears, arms, hands, a back, or a nose? Only the fringes of the church have ever thought God to have a physical body (outside the Incarnation), and yet there are many verses that seem to say he is physical. Why should we deny the corporeality of God? Well, because we know that we are not marginalising these texts by reading them as *anthropomorphisms*, as ways of speaking in human figures to teach us about God's character or action without actually making God physical. Let's be consistent with 'emotional' texts.

Furthermore, in light of the diversity of Scripture, we all make synthesising decisions, based on a range of considerations. In the realm of impassibility, this is clearly seen in 1 Sam 15.

After Saul's transgression of God's command, God 'regrets' that he made Saul king (15:11, 35). However, it is also said of God that he does not lie or have regret because he is *not* a man (15:29). Making sense of this requires accounting for the different contexts in which the seemingly contradictory statements occur. First, God's regret that he has made Saul king is made in response to Saul's own actions, and the unfolding drama of God's redemptive kingdom. As the people progress along the course, they find that God is actively involved in the process; we might say that this text describes the grittiness of covenantal interaction. Second, the statement that God does *not* have regret is expressly couched in the context of the *contrast* between God and humanity. That is, it represents a more direct statement about what God is like (actually, what he is *not* like), and therefore can be given 'priority' when making decisions about God's nature. This is only the beginning of an answer, but you can start to see how the bigger biblical picture needs to be carefully read as a whole to make sense of what each part might, or might not, be saying.

## Isn't it enough to say that God's sovereign will never changes?

Some recent evangelical proposals have changed the doctrine of God to introduce separate parts into God's existence. In different ways they all want to say that God's sovereign will doesn't change, but that another part of God or his experience does.

This is not a better option. First, the relationship between God's being and his will that is introduced is problematic. The reason why impassibility and immutability have been such a comfort is that God's unchangingness, and insusceptibility to external pressure or mood swings, is not based in a *decision* that he has made, but in a glorious *inability* to change in any way. If God's being, however, is subject to change, then why is there a guarantee that God's will won't?

In addition, we are back to a problem common to any account of God changing. If God undergoes emotional change at some level then we undermine, rather than establish, our ability to relate to him. If he really responds differently to different things, undergoing real emotional change in interaction with someone in, say, Manchester, then surely such change has a real effect. How does this affect God's interaction with someone else in Cardiff? Does God, in Cardiff, absorb the emotional change caused in Manchester, and thus change during someone's prayer in South Wales? If not, how is it the same God? When multiplied by the number of people in creation, and spread across time, then precisely with whom are we relating when we engage with God? Or indeed, if God is really experiencing this level of relational change all the time, he must be engaged in an "unending internal emotional whirligig."

*ibid.*, 163

Instead, believing that God is fully active in his relational activity as Father, Son, and Spirit, the traditional account is able to say that God does not need to undergo change in order to fully relate to whomever is in Manchester, Cardiff, or Kampala, whenever they might be found. His revealed effects of love really make a difference to us, even without bringing about difference in him. Because God's love is wholly in act, he is "immutably and impassibly adapted to every situation and circumstance, not because his love is indifferent and unresponsive, but because his love, with all its facets, is fully in act, and so he is supremely and utterly responsive to every situation and circumstance."

*ibid.*, 163

## *Incarnation*

Of course, the incarnation and suffering of God the Son may, initially, represent a challenge to divine impassibility in a simple formula: (1) Jesus suffers; (2) Jesus is God; therefore (3) God suffers.

However, it was belief in impassibility alongside a firm commitment to the real suffering of Christ and his full incarnation as a true man, that led the early church to be as precise as it was in formulating its Christological statements. In the Chalcedonian Definition of 451, the impassibility of the Son's divine nature is expressly preserved. The solution – to recognise the union of two natures in the one person of the Son – allows a robust affirmation that on the cross we see the redemptive suffering of God. The communication of properties of both natures to the one person, a useful Chalcedonian tool, explains how Scripture speaks of the "blood of God" (Acts 20) in the sense that God (the Son) is the person *to whom* human blood belongs, but by virtue of his human nature. It was indeed God (the Son) *who* suffered, *who* wept, *who* died in our place for our redemption; but it was God *as a man* that did so. His weeping and emotions represent the perfect moral character of God, no longer *as if* he were under the conditions of time, space, and corporeality, but as he *actually is* under those conditions as a true man.

*This* is the Christian good news of the suffering God, and the richest expression of his impassible love. Our comfort is not that *God* suffers *with* us, but that God *as a man* suffered *for* us, securing victory over that very suffering through resurrection. Indeed, a vague sense of God suffering as God is of no real help, as Todd Billings observes:

> *The notion of God-as-Spirit suffering in a non-bodily or nonhuman way provides me [a cancer sufferer] no solace, no companionship, no identification. I believe that God knows me in my suffering, with a perfect, loving intimacy. But to say 'God suffers with me' leaves me isolated in my bodily suffering.*

From 'Undying Love' on *firstthings.com*. See also his *Rejoicing in Lament: Wrestling with Incurable Cancer & Life in Christ* (Grand Rapids, MI.: Brazos, 2015), 149-167, for a beautiful account of impassibility's comfort.

As God, the Son could not suffer, and the incarnation itself is pointless if he could do so. In fact, this is the logic behind Hebrews 2. In order to become our high priest and be qualified to atone for our sins through suffering, the Son had to partake of our own flesh and blood (Heb 2:10, 14-18). The cross does not reveal eternal suffering in God, but accomplishes purposeful redemption. Christ's sympathy as high priest (4:15) comes from his necessarily *human* mission.

See Kevin DeYoung, 'Divine Impassibility and the Passion of Christ in the Book of Hebrews,' *WTJ*, 68 (2006): 41-50.

# IMPASSIBILITY AND PASTORAL MINISTRY

This attribute of God plays a vital role in pastoral ministry; this *true* teaching is also *helpful*.

## Idolatry

We have already considered the stability of promise-keeping that can only be guaranteed by divine impassibility, but it is always worth remembering that when the gospel is held out, the God behind it is beyond the possibility of manipulation or whimsy. He is not fickle like the idols.

However, our hearts are prone to some serious idol construction precisely because we are drawn to the familiarity of a fickle person, made in our image, who can be controlled. Divine impassibility unsettles those hearts by reminding us that God is beyond that. We want to think that his love must be like our own, that his experience must be like our own, and therefore that he really is like us after all. The traditional doctrine of God, with its robust denial of all that is creaturely in God, and in particular with its recognition that God's infinitely realised love is simply beyond the conniving grasp of our presumptuous efforts at manipulation, stands as a stern warning against pathetic views of our Maker and Redeemer.

## Human suffering

So, the transcendence of God helps us to relate to God rightly in piety and worship. It also helps think more clearly about how to relate to him in suffering.

First, as others have noted, the desire for someone else to share in my misery can start to treat their suffering as a *good* thing. And yet, it is not. We do not get comfort from having others join in our suffering. Rather, it is when our friends or family come alongside to do us good.

When my daughter falls over, I do not slump down next to her, lean against her, and cry along. My fatherly love means that I am able to smile, sweep her up, and hug her tightly in safe arms. It is true, there are times when we see our children suffering that we feel the pain inside ourselves, but this happens at exactly those moments when we are powerless to make everything better. The more powerless in relation to our beloved's suffering, the more pain we feel; indeed, this is part of what it means to be a creature, weeping with those who weep.

Second, to have a suffering God is exactly the opposite of what sufferers needs. We don't want a God who has aspirations of reaching a suffering-free existence: if he is eternally subject to suffering we cannot trust him to get us out of it! We don't need a Father who slumps alongside us weeping too. In the sickness of our sin, we don't need a doctor who says, "it's okay, I've got a disease as well!"

Instead, we need an all-sufficient Saviour who is powerful to do all that he wants, whose commitment to his children is unwavering; who, because he is outside the created order, is able to act within it with saving power without losing anything of himself in doing so. Such a God can supply significance to our suffering in locating it within a larger sovereign plan in which our present "light and momentary troubles are achieving for us an eternal glory that far outweighs them all" (2 Cor 4:17).

Third, a passible God not only lacks the *ability* to overcome and vanquish suffering forever, but also the guaranteed *motivation* to do so. Remember, we don't merely trust that God has made a decision not to be coerced emotionally; he is not *capable* of it. But what if he was able to achieve better for himself by breaking his promises? What we need in our suffering is not a God whose shifting emotional states make it possible that he could act in his own self-interest because he gets something out of us. Grace would no longer be grace. But since God is impassible, nothing you do impairs or improves his life. So he is free to make all the difference in the world to you.

Eternal life is knowing God (John 17:3) and enjoying life as adopted children in the eternal love of Father and Son in the Holy Spirit, but if that love contains the possibility of pain and fracture, what kind of paradise is really on offer? Divine impassibility confirms the infinite blessedness of the God who is not only the ground, but the goal of the gospel itself.

# A PERSONAL NOTE

In closing, I want to talk about how I have personally received comfort from the reality of God's impassibility. Now, a doctrine is not true because it's helpful, and if you're worried that I'm going to rely on my experience as an argument, I'd refer you to the rest of the article above. God must be like this if the Bible is true.

However, precisely because it is true, it has been a real help to me, and maybe your concerns about the deployment of divine impassibility in pastoral ministry can be seriously diluted, if not dismissed altogether, by my own story.

In October 2015, our daughter, Talitha, died aged three. She had serious epilepsy and a chest full of arteries that should not have been there, caused by a rare genetic condition. These vessels began bursting in her lungs, and it ended up being fatal.

Convinced of God's covenant mercies, and the joy Tilly had in hearing the gospel read, prayed, and sung, we are confident that one day she will hear Jesus' words in Mark 5:41 spoken with eschatological power: "'Talitha, cumi', which means 'little girl, I say to you, arise.'" Our hope is in a world in which tears are no more, and we look forward to an everlasting delight in enjoying the blessedness of the triune God with his people. The unwavering certainty of this promise, held out in Scripture, is founded on a God of unwavering disposition and decree, one who *cannot* be moved in his infinite love.

But there's even more specific help than that. The first time she had a serious bleed in her lungs was the time we discovered just how terrible her situation was. She was rushed into ICU, and during her stay there we went from terror, to joy, and back again, as she suffered various crashes, procedures to put things right, further problems with helping her breathe on her own again (including a fraught disagreement with medical staff about her future), until finally she was better and able to come home. Despite my dislike for cliché, I can only describe the experience as a two-week emotional rollercoaster, and we were utterly ruined at the end of it. And one kindly soul remarked "well at least you know God went through it with you."

Now, we received that word with the kindness with which it was intended; it was hardly the place to speak about the simple pure actuality of the triune God. Nevertheless, I was struck by the phrase "God went through it with you." The response in my head was "I really flipping hope not." I was a wreck, an absolute mess, an emotional disaster. It was not comforting to consider God feeling the same way! The good news is not that God went through it with me; the good news is that God was with me as *I* went through it, and precisely because of his impassibility he was free to be close to me and sustain me with grace in an embrace of love so indestructible that nothing could get in its way.

It seems to me that Bavinck gets it just right:

*Those who predicate any change whatsoever of God, whether with respect to his essence, knowledge, or will, diminish all his attributes: independence, simplicity, eternity, omniscience, and omnipotence. This robs God of his divine nature, and religion of its firm foundation and assured comfort.*

Herman Bavinck, *Reformed Dogmatics (4 Vols)* (trans. John Vriend; Grand Rapids, MI.: Baker, 2004), 2:158.

# FURTHER READING

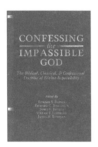

### Confessing the Impassible God
#### Edited by Ronald Baines & others

A collection of essays, published by Reformed Baptists, which define and defend divine impassibility. Four hundred pages means a stretching but well-argued case.

### Does God Suffer?
#### Thomas Weinandy

Weinandy is a Roman Catholic, whose seminal work on divine impassibility is justifiably admired by many in our circles.

For chapter-length treatments, see Peter Sanlon's *Simply God*, Garry Williams' *His Love Endures Forever*, and Matthew Barrett's new book *None Greater: The Undomesticated Attributes of God*.

## Questions for further thought and discussion

1. Chris wrote that "Impassibility does not deny joy, delight, and love in God. It attributes those things to God without the limitations and imperfections that attach to them when present in us." Have a go at putting in your own words what impassibility does rule out then:

   *God's love is not...*

2. One of the claims of this article is that God's impassibility is a great comfort in the face of suffering. Read James 1:1-18. How does James teach Christians facing trials to think about God's nature, and their own? How does he express the difference between God and fallen human beings?

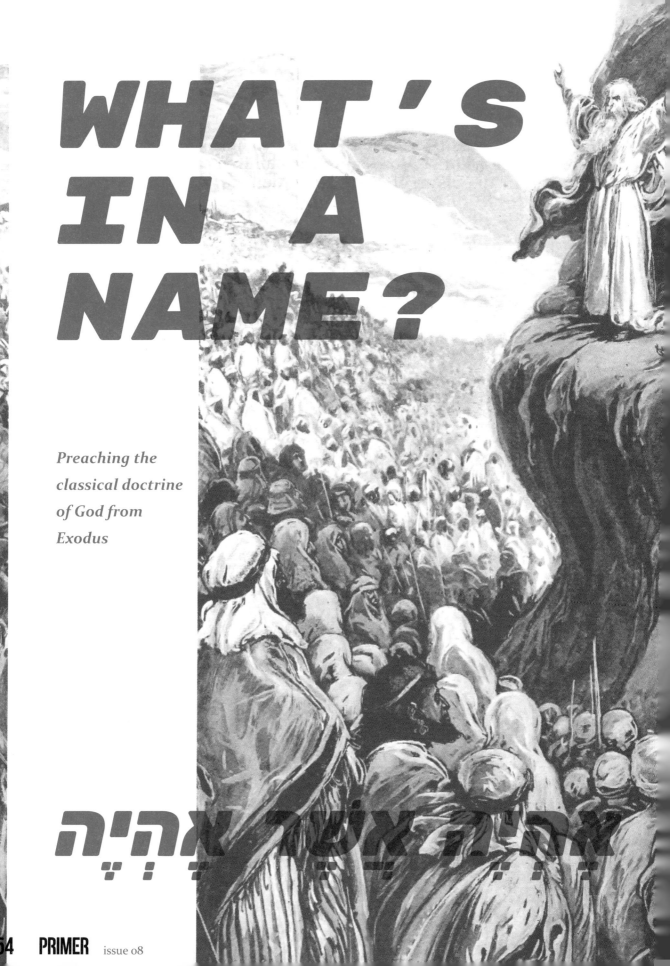

# WHAT'S IN A NAME?

*Preaching the classical doctrine of God from Exodus*

אֶהְיֶה אֲשֶׁר אֶהְיֶה

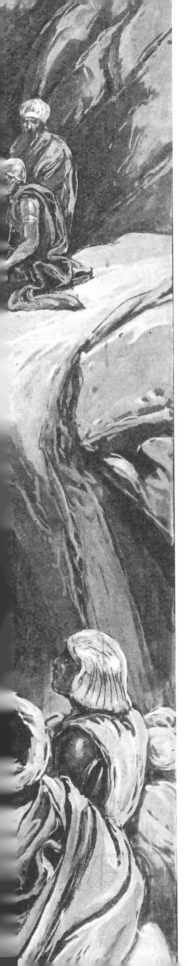

**SAMUEL BOSTOCK** trained for gospel ministry at St Helen's, Bishopsgate in London and Union Theological College in Belfast. He now serves as assistant minister at Bloomfield Presbyterian Church, which meets on Cyprus Avenue in East Belfast.

 @sambostock

**If we are going to preach the doctrine of God, Exodus is surely the place to do it. Quite clearly, God brought his people out of Egypt so that** *"they will know that I am the LORD their God"* **(Exod 29:46). Exodus is a foundational book in the canon of Scripture, both as a description of salvation, and as a description of the God who saves.**

But in practice it is surprisingly easy to preach Exodus and avoid the kind of discussions about the classical doctrine of God that we have been having in *Primer*. Indeed, I have happily preached my way through Exodus twice before without concerning myself with the doctrine of God's simplicity. "God reveals himself by what he does," I said to myself, "so I don't need to get into all the nitty-gritty. Just preach the passage and we will get to know God as he wants us to."

This instinct raises a question that many of us may have. The classical doctrine of God may all be well and good. But is it practical? Is it relevant for the ordinary believer? If the classical doctrine of God is relevant, then surely it must not be ivory-tower speculation, but fall out of the passages that the Lord has given us to preach. So the question is: does the classical doctrine of God really preach? My answer from my most recent experience preaching through Exodus is an emphatic 'yes!'

I want to suggest in this article that *expository preaching from Exodus pushes us towards, and benefits from, the classical doctrine of God*. It may be helpful to think of this article as a sort of 'from text to sermon' piece that emphasises one sometimes overlooked stage – the role of systematic theology in drawing out the meaning and relevance of the Scripture.

## I. THE CALL TO WORSHIP IN EXODUS 3:1-12

Exodus does not present the doctrine of God in the form of a systematic theology. Rather, Exodus leads its hearers on a journey towards fuller knowledge of God. Physically, the LORD takes Israel on a journey in the first half of the book (Exod 1-18) from the swampy floodplains of idolatrous Egypt to a meeting with God in the sky-blue mountain air of Sinai. The second half (Exod 19-40) then describes how the one who dwells on the mountain of God descends to go with his covenant people on the journey to the new mountain of God: Zion (cf. Exod 15:12-16). As we follow Moses and Israel making this physical journey towards God we join them in making a parallel spiritual journey towards a true understanding of the incomparable power of the LORD (Exod 1-18), and towards a true understanding of his justice and mercy (Exod 19-40).

Before either of these journeys can begin we are taken away to a mountain for an encounter with the LORD himself at the burning bush in Exod 3. This encounter serves as an orientation to the journey to come. We will focus on three crucial lessons (two in this section, one in the next).

The first lesson comes from the location of this encounter. Moses is leading the flocks of his father-in-law through the wilderness, and comes to a place that is designated already as "the mountain of God" (Exod 3:1). The reason for this designation shortly becomes clear, with the LORD declaring that "when you have brought the people out of Egypt, you will worship God on this mountain" (Exod 3:12). The exit from Egypt will not be aimless, but will result in Israel gathering at Sinai to worship in the LORD's presence, just as Moses does now. Insofar as Exodus lays out the basic pattern of God's salvation, we learn that this salvation is not merely sourced from God or resourced by God but terminates in an assembly of people coming *to* God as their destination. Preachers should take note: we must not preach milk and honey but God as the goal of our salvation.

The second lesson begins as Moses moves across to investigate this strange sight. A burning bush was presumably not an unusual occurrence in the Arabian Desert. But this bush burns, and is not burned up! So Moses approaches to "look" more closely – and a voice from the bush instructs him to proceed no further, and to take off his sandals. Although the LORD moves quickly to comfort Moses, introducing himself as "the God of your father" (Exod 3:6), at no point are we informed that Moses moves any closer. Instead, Moses hides his face, "afraid to look at God" (Exod 3:7).

Everything suggests that this is an exemplary response. Moses now rightly appreciates that the bush is not open to investigation like a natural phenomenon. He takes off his sandals, for it is holy ground. Having understood the significance of the spectacle, Moses gives up his "bold and curious searching into God's secrets" (*Westminster Larger Catechism*, Q. 105) and adopts a posture of humility. Further revelation in this episode comes only through speech.

This movement, from a bold and curious desire to see to a denial of sight to a certain limited kind of revelation, is repeated again in Exodus. In chapter 33:18-20 Moses asks to see God's glory. The LORD refuses, for "no-one can see my face and live." The LORD promises instead to cause "all his goodness" to pass in front of Moses – but only once Moses has purified himself. The report of the resulting encounter in the next chapter gives absolutely no visual description of God, providing instead a detailed account of the LORD's *proclamation* of his goodness, which we shall consider more fully below.

The suggestion here is that in these two episodes the Holy Spirit is teaching us something fundamental about how we approach the doctrine of God. We must move from approaching God as just another object of investigation to a more appropriate attitude. As Gregory of Nazianzus says, the doctrine of God is not for everyone, "but only for those who... have undergone, or at the very least are undergoing, purification of body and soul." Since our hearts are, in Calvin's famous summary, "factories of idols", gaining true knowledge of God will often involve much unlearning of what we think we know, in order to receive the LORD's own revelation of himself. We should expect that learning to think of God will require humility and resolute attentiveness to the particular ways that the LORD chooses to make himself known, for the place where we are standing is holy ground. Genuine preaching of the knowledge of God will stretch both preacher and congregation. But if God is the goal of our salvation then it cannot be avoided.

Gregory of Nazianzus, *Oration 27*, in *On God and Christ: The Five Theological Orations and Two Letters to Cledonius* (Crestwood, New York: St Vladimir's Seminary Press, 2002), 27.

## II. GOD'S NAME REVEALED IN EXODUS 3:13-14

Once the introductions have taken place, the LORD outlines his plan to rescue his people from Egypt. Surprisingly he concludes by including Moses: "So now, go. I am sending you to Pharaoh to bring my people the Israelites out of Egypt" (Exod 3:10). Somewhat taken aback, Moses raises five objections. The LORD's answers to these all refer Moses back the LORD's own self-sufficiency. We take our third lesson from the second objection, in which God gives the meaning of his name, the LORD. Moses asks, "If I go and tell the sons of Israel that God has sent me, and they ask me 'what is his name?' what should I say?" It is worth remembering that names in Scripture are not normally arbitrary labels: they usually reflect the nature of a thing. Since God has already identified himself as "the God of your father", Moses' request for God to give his name should be understood as a request for God to reveal something of his nature.

The LORD responds: "I AM WHO I AM" (Exod 3:14). This phrase is the combination of two instances of the normal Hebrew verb for existence (*to be*), in a form that could refer to past, present or future, joined by the

Grammatically, it is an imperfect tense in Hebrew, but this could be translated in various ways.

WE MUST NOT PREACH MILK AND HONEY BUT GOD AS THE GOAL OF OUR SALVATION relative particle (who/what). We might translate it variously as "I am what I am" or "I will be who I will be" or "I will be who I am", etc.

Many of us might be tempted to skip quickly over this enigmatic phrase. After all, it is just three words in Hebrew, and we have a lot to cover in this passage. But the name that derives from this statement, YHWH (normally rendered in English translations in capitals as *the* LORD), will be used more than 6,800 times in the Old Testament. This passage shows it is not a place holder, to be filled out by God's actions in history. Rather, this name has a definite content that conditions our understanding of God's actions in history.

YHWH are the Hebrew consonants usually pronounced 'Yahweh' (the name Jehovah also comes from this root).

So what does the phrase mean? The **Septuagint** translates the Hebrew "I am what I am" as something like "I am the one who is" (ἐγώ εἰμι ὁ ὤν) or "I am the Being." The impact of this translation can be seen in many of the church fathers, who regularly call God "He Who Is."

The Septuagint refers to a translation of the Old Testament into Greek widely used in the New Testament era. Traditionally, it was the work of 72 translators, hence Septuagint (which means seventy) and the abbreviation LXX.

For example, Augustine, Gregory of Nazianzus and John of Damascus.

But many biblical scholars see the Septuagint translation as an example of the *Hellenization Thesis*. That is, the idea that the Hebrew Bible, concerned with God's relationship to his people, is polluted by a Greek preoccupation with questions about the essence of existence and being.

This idea dates back to Adolf von Harnack (1851-1930). His *History of Dogma* was built around the thesis that the original gospel of Jesus was a moral teaching, which became twisted into a more abstract scheme of salvation by the later encounter with Greek philosophy.

As a result, many people are wary of interpreting God's statement that "I AM WHAT I AM" as if it speaks of God's nature or being. One common option is to read the LORD as saying "I will be [with you]." But apart from the fact that this would merely be a repetition of the answer to the first objection (Exod 3:12), this interpretation fails to recognise that "I am what I am" seems to be deliberately setting up a kind of circularity, in which nothing external is allowed to enter into the definition of the LORD's name. Alternatively, some suggest that the LORD is simply refusing Moses' request on the grounds of impertinence. "I am who I am, and I'm not telling you!"

Others think the LORD is delaying defining himself, instead promising to reveal himself through his saving acts. "I will be who I will be, and you'll see as soon as I start smiting Egypt."

But both of these interpretations are broken on the rock of the second half of the LORD's reply: "This is what you are to say to the Israelites: 'I AM has sent me to you'" (Exod 3:14). The two versions of the name demand to be read together. The longer version does emphasise circularity, a refusal to be named. But the shorter version seems to offer a kind of intelligibility. The message to Israel is not "An unknown entity has sent me to you" but a far more positive statement: "*I AM* has sent me to you."

If we return to the Hebrew phrase itself, can we draw any firm conclusions? The conclusion of the vast majority of Christian, not to say Jewish, exegetes is that there are two foundational truths about God that really sit on the surface of this statement, however much we struggle to comprehend them.

First, the tradition concurs with modern exegetes that there is a certain refusal by God to submit to creaturely naming. But God does not simply refuse to name himself. Rather, he refuses to name himself by reference to any other being, whether on heaven or on earth. God can only name himself *by himself*. The point is that God is in a class by himself. There is none like him. Any description of him in terms taken from creation will prove finally insufficient. Instead, Exod 3:14 reveals that the LORD is the one who is from and for himself. This first truth corresponds to the traditional *via negativa*, the negative way. To come to knowledge of God we must strip away everything creaturely from our thoughts.

But Exod 3:14 also teaches us a second, more positive way of speaking about God. This in particular comes from the shorter version of the name: I AM. Here circularity is less obvious; the emphasis now falls on the verb ('am'). Unfortunately the common decision of English translators to render these words in upper case, combined with the way the verb 'to be' changes form radically when conjugated in English, has slightly hidden the obvious point. It becomes clearer, though, when we recognise that the one who declares himself to be 'I AM' can equally be called 'He *is*', or, in personal address, 'You *are*.' According to T. D. Alexander in his authoritative new commentary on Exodus, this is precisely what happens with the word YHWH. This name is derived from the third person form of the verb 'to be.' At the burning bush the LORD calls himself "I AM", and forever he wants us to call him "He is." Instead of resisting a metaphysical understanding of God's name, Exodus invites it. Scripture urges us to join the fathers in confessing the truth that God really is the One Who *Is*.

T. Desmond Alexander, *Exodus* (London: Apollos, 2017), 90.

One final observation draws these two points together. In ordinary language, when we want to say what something is we always include a predicate. Suzy is *a sheep*. A human being is *a rational animal*. The predicate serves to identify the particular kind of being that the subject is. But in the second half of Exod 3:14 God does not complete the sentence – he just *is*. The significance of this grammatical failure is monumental. In one way, we could say that in the singular case of God, there is no predicate that can successfully identify the LORD as a particular kind of being. Not even an infinite combination of the glories of the various different creaturely ways of being could ever adequately describe the sheer fullness of being that God is. Alternatively, we could say that the LORD needs no further description to pick out his particular kind of being. *What* he is (his 'essence') is the same as *that* he is (his 'existence'). The LORD alone irreducibly, concretely and inexpressibly is, for he declares to Moses that he is not a being among beings, but pure unbounded being itself.

Here's how I attempted to preach this understanding of Exod 3:14:

*Normally if we want to say what something is, we can give them a definition. Suzy is a sheep. Rebecca is a rabbit, and so on. But we can't do that to God. We can't define him. He is what he is. He doesn't fit into any category. The best we can do is just to stop short. God is not this and this and this. He simply is.*

*When we say somebody is, we're saying something fairly basic. Somebody could exist, and have a very limited existence – something could be an amoeba and exist. But when we say God is, we're saying that if we say any more, we'll actually end up limiting God by using some kind of created category to define him. Even if we could add up every good thing in this universe, everything that is, we would still not get anywhere close to talking about all that God is.*

With these observations we have arrived at the basic affirmations of the classical doctrine of God. For an example from the Latin tradition, here is the noted medieval exegete Nicolas of Lyra's summary of how Exod 3:14 teaches us to think of God: "He who has the necessity and fullness of being from himself without any restriction or determination." This is not just a medieval doctrine, however. From almost a millennium earlier, here is the Cappadocian Gregory of Nazianzus: "Holding everything together in himself, he possesses being, neither beginning nor ending. He is like a kind of boundless and limitless sea of being, surpassing all thought and time and nature."

Quoted in Stephen E. Fowl, ed., *The Theological Interpretation of Scripture: Classic and Contemporary Readings* (Oxford: Blackwell, 1997), 23.

Gregory of Nazianzus, *Oration 38: On the Nativity of Christ*, in *Festal Orations*, trans. Nonna Vera Harrison (Crestwood, New York: St Vladimir's Seminary Press, 2008), 65.

With this understanding of God's name in place, one could, with enough time, derive the various traditional perfections of God, such as simplicity, aseity, eternity and infinity. For example, John Owen summarises God's name as "I AM; I AM THAT I AM", and then draws the implications for the doctrine of God's simplicity: "He then, who is what he is, and whose all that is in him is himself, hath neither parts, accidents, principles, nor anything else, whereof his essence should be compounded." If the only way we can say what God is, is to say that he simply is what he is, then he is pure existence and not composed of any more basic parts.

John Owen, *Works: volume 12* (Edinburgh: Banner of Truth, 1966), 72.

But not everyone is convinced that Moses was given access to such mind-bending ideas. The Reformed biblical theologian Geerhardus Vos shrewdly articulates a sense that many of us may share. Although it is possible that "pure being" is what the name means, he says, "it is far too abstract an idea to be suitable here." Surely Moses could hardly be expected to spend time contemplating the beauties of the infinite, when he had a people to lead out of slavery. By the same token, of what benefit is it to ask our congregations to follow us in some fairly abstract metaphysical thought when we have the gospel to proclaim?

Geerhardus Vos, *Biblical Theology: Old and New Testaments* (Edinburgh: Banner of Truth, 1975), 118.

But to ask these questions suggests that we have not learnt the first lesson of the burning bush. God is the goal of our salvation. And so a properly metaphysical view of the meaning of the name is precisely what we need. Historically speaking, the Israelites were in the grip of idolatry. If the LORD is going to make himself known to his people, he had to start by teaching them that he is not merely stronger than the idols of Egypt (Exod 4-12) but qualitatively different to them. To be sure, this word would have required contemplation. But it seems to me that Moses and Israel had time enough for that when marching through the desert. Soon Moses would show that he has learned the truth of God's incomparability: "Who among the gods is like you, LORD? Who is like you?" (Exod 15:11). Canonically speaking, this explanation of the name occurs very early in both Exodus and Scripture, giving us a kind of key to understanding all subsequent descriptions of God rightly: every time we read *the LORD*, we are invited to remember that he is The One Who Is, to recall the encounter at the burning bush, and to have our thoughts about God reformed.

Here is how I sought to apply this:

*I would love for you to take this name, and let it seep into your mind and how you think about God. I think we are meant to take this name into our Bible reading, and allow it to reshape how we think about God. Think of a hot air balloon. They are always prone to drifting down. We're always prone to making God like us. Calvin says very helpfully, 'our hearts are factories of idols' – we are always prone to making God in our image. But this name is like the burner in a hot air balloon. I am what I am. Every time you think about God and you start bringing him down to your level, which you have to do if you are going to think about God at all, at the same time, you need to flick on the burner, and allow your thoughts about God to rise back up again, to something approaching all that God is.*

In the next section we will see how the traditional understanding of God's name helps us to preach God's power as good news.

## III. A GENEROUS GLORY IN EXODUS 14-15

After the battle of the Red Sea, Moses sings:

> **Exod 15:2** | *The LORD is my strength and my song, he has become my salvation.*

I am following the reading in the footnote of the NIV2011 text. The main text replaces 'song' (NIV1984) with 'defence.'

This is a good summary of what the first section of Exodus has taught us about God. The LORD has kept his covenant promises by saving his people with a mighty hand and an outstretched arm. And it is a venerable and basic part of the Christian confession: We believe in one God, the Father Almighty. But Moses' joy also raises a challenge for the preacher. I do not know what it was like in Constantinople in the 4th century, but congregations in Belfast today do not necessarily feel like singing when they read about God smiting the Egyptians. They sometimes form the impression that the LORD is acting in these chapters like a playground bully who is trying to assert his authority, and crushing anyone who gets in his way. This sense might be exacerbated by reading that in advance of the Egyptians drowning the Lord declared,

The first line of the Nicene Creed, amended and approved at a church council in Constantinople in A.D.381.

> **Exod 14:4** | *"I will harden Pharaoh's heart, and he will pursue them. But I will gain glory for myself through Pharaoh and all his army, and the Egyptians will know that I am the LORD."*

Sure enough, after the LORD drowns the men of Egypt, Moses begins to praise him. It rather starts to look as though God benefits from drowning Pharaoh. Or even needs him as a pawn in order to get glory.

Here is an example of how the name of the LORD can help to purify our thinking about God. If we think of God as simply the greatest among many powers, then power and glory will be a zero-sum game: God can only be the winner if others are the losers. But if God is what he is, then he is self-sufficient and his strength is not affected by anything beside himself, because he simply is not on the same plane of being. Rather than being the most powerful force in the universe, the encounter at the burning bush suggests the LORD is better described as the being that energises our universe. There is no power or might that is not in some way *his* power, *his* might. This is what it means to say that he is the Almighty.

And so God's strength is not exerted out of any need to prove himself. In fact, the traditional understanding of God's name implies that God can't get glory from us. He is what he is so he can't be augmented or improved in any way by creation. Why then did God create the world? "God wills [other things from himself] not to increase, but to diffuse his goodness."

(*diffuse* = to spread out, or distribute) Francis Turretin, *Institutes of Elenctic Theology* (Phillipsburg: Presbyterian and Reformed, 1992), 1:220. See also *Westminster Confession of Faith*, 2.2; Thomas Aquinas, *Summa Theologiae* 1a.19.2 and 1a.44.4: "*He alone is the most liberal giver, because He does not act for his own profit, but only for his own goodness.*"

According to this doctrine of God, whatever is happening when the LORD "gets glory", it cannot be for his benefit. Who then benefits when God "gets glory"? In Exod 15 the answer is obvious: God's people. With their backs against the Red Sea, Moses and the people are terrified. They urgently need to learn to trust God – now, and in the future, as he leads them through the desert. So the LORD determines to "get glory" over Pharaoh: he wills to display something of his limitless power by parting the Red Sea and returning it to its place. When their pursuers are washed up on the shore the people put their trust in God and begin to sing. Not to a playground bully, but to the God who is genuinely incomparable:

*Exod 15:11*

> Who among the gods is like you, LORD? Who is like you – majestic in holiness, awesome in glory, working wonders?

A metaphysical understanding of the name of God helps us to see that God's strength is good news. Because he alone is the One Who Is, the majestically holy LORD "gets glory" not for himself but in order to give a saving vision of his glory to his people.

# IV. GOD'S GOODNESS ON DISPLAY IN EXODUS 33-34

Some readers may be concerned that in the previous section the classical doctrine of God has ridden roughshod over what seems to be the plain meaning of Exodus 14:4, that God will gain glory for himself. In this final section I will make some brief comments on the climactic episode of Exodus, and perhaps of the entire Old Testament: the encounter with the LORD on Sinai in Exod 33-34. This will support our earlier reading of Exod 14-15, and illustrate further how the classical doctrine of God can sharpen up our reading of the text.

After the great sin of the golden calf, Moses emerges as the only blameless Israelite. After receiving confirmation that the LORD will go with him as he leads the people to the promised land, Moses seeks one thing more of the LORD: he asks to see God's glory. Taken as a request to see God's face, this is denied, as we saw above. But the LORD does promise to "cause all my goodness to pass in front of you, and I will proclaim my name, the LORD, in your presence" (Exod 33:19).

This comment clarifies what is about to take place. First, Moses is being offered a limited, creaturely, but genuine revelation of God. Moses is not in a position to see God's face (traditionally associated with God's exhaustive knowledge of God's nature or 'essence'), but God will *cause* all his goodness to pass before Moses. Although the "all" is not offering exhaustive revelation of God's goodness, it is promising appropriately comprehensive knowledge. Second, this revelation will display the LORD's "goodness." Presumably this is not to suggest that the LORD has a dark side that he is unwilling to display but rather that goodness characterises all that God is. Just so, the traditional doctrine teaches that God is, and his being simply is sheer unfathomable goodness.

E.g. John Owen: "This is the first notion of the divine nature, - infinite being and goodness, in a nature intelligent and self-subsistent." Works: vol 1 (Edinburgh: Banner of Truth, 1966), 368. Cf. John of Damascus, *On the Orthodox Faith*, 1.9; Thomas Aquinas, *Summa Theologiae*, 1a.3-6.

The next day, Moses presents himself at the top of Sinai and when the LORD comes down in the cloud to meet him, Moses "called on the name of the LORD" (Exod 34:5, my translation). Placing Moses in a cleft in a rock, the LORD's glory then passes in front of Moses, as he proclaims:

**Exod 34:6-7**
> The LORD, the LORD, the compassionate and gracious God, slow to anger, abounding in love and faithfulness, maintaining love to thousands, and forgiving wickedness, rebellion and sin. Yet he does not leave the guilty unpunished; he punishes the children and their children for the sin of the parents to the third and fourth generation.

Earlier we emphasised that properly speaking the LORD only receives glory in order to give a saving vision of his glory to his people. Here, at the very peak of the Exodus story, we see that this emphasis is true to the dramatic thrust of Exodus. After the nightmare of the Golden Calf (Exod 32), and before his glory fills the tabernacle (Exod 40), God graciously grants Moses, and us, an intimate description of his glory. This is the reward for those who have journeyed with Moses from the mountain of God and back again.

As we have noted already, this revelation is not so much in visual as verbal form. In Scripture we "see" the LORD with our minds, not with our eyes. So what do we see?

First, we see the LORD's self-sufficient goodness. The repetition of the LORD's name recalls the burning bush: "He is, He is." Because he is what he is, mercy and grace proceeds from the closed circle of the LORD's inner goodness: "I will have mercy on whom I will have mercy, and I will have compassion on whom I will have compassion" (Exod 33:19).

Second, we see the LORD's varied ways of making his goodness known. We are perhaps inclined to think of the glowing qualities described in the verses above as a set of 'attributes' of God – descriptions of God's perfect nature. But Moses' inability to see God's "face" should make us hesitate. And what might it mean for "slowness" to anger to be a description of what God is? How slow to anger must one be to be perfect? We are helped by making a distinction between God's inner being and his outer works. According to the classical doctrine of God, the qualities in the verses above are attributes of God only in the sense that they are summary descriptions of God's consistent ways of working in the world. The LORD is proclaiming to Moses how he will *cause* his goodness to pass before us in the world. Like a shaft of light splitting into multiple rays as it comes through a prism, so the LORD's simple being must have diverse effects in creation if we are to begin to grasp its fullness. On this account, the LORD's various acts of both mercy and judgment help us to grasp something of his utterly pure inner goodness. So the LORD's slowness to anger does not reveal that God has a kind of inner fuse that happens to be longer than other people's. Rather, God's slowness to anger is an outward effect: the LORD regularly delays punishment for sin. This pattern of working reveals something of God's inner goodness: it remains unaffected and unthreatened by our sin, even as it works to remove it according to the LORD's good pleasure.

Our concern in this article has been to see whether expository preaching of Exodus might benefit from engagement with the classical doctrine of God. I hope to have shown that it does. Although there is inevitably something of a circular relationship between doctrine and exegesis, we have seen that the traditional affirmation of God's aseity is rooted in God's own self-description. Although this vocabulary will not be appropriate for the pulpit, the finely-tooled grammar of the classical doctrine can be used, like the divine name that it explores, to bring clarity in preaching texts that sometimes strain under the height and weight and length and depth of the glory of the God of Israel. Although I can't be sure that I successfully passed that clarity onto my hearers, I have certainly benefited from it myself in preparation. And I believe this investment in doctrinal thinking is not really optional if the preacher wants to cut with the grain of the text.

Perhaps more than any other part of Scripture, Exodus aids us in our salvation by leading us away from the soul-destroying lure of idolatry towards the living God. Our prayer must be that Exodus would help our preaching to do the same.

## Questions for further thought and discussion

1. In recent Bible teaching, how have issues of systematic theology arisen and how have you reflected on them? How does your church equip people to do that?

2. When God reveals himself as the "I AM," it is a signal that "he is like a kind of boundless and limitless sea of being, surpassing all thought and time and nature" (Gregory of Nazianzus). How does Sam argue that from Exodus?

   How does that increase a sense of wonder that the Word became flesh and dwelt amongst us, naming himself as the "I AM"? (John 8:58, 18:6)

3. How does Sam's distinction between God's *inner goodness* and its *outward effects* help us understand how God's people experience him? Where else has this distinction been useful in this issue?

**MATT LILLICRAP** lives in Cambridge where he is the Associate Pastor at Eden Baptist Church. Previously he worked as a medical registrar in Hospital medicine before heading to Oak Hill College as an Independent student. He is married to Anika and they have six children aged between 3 and 10.

 *@MHLillicrap*

Pastoral
Ministry &
the Creator-
Creature
Distinction

# re-placing humanity

# "Who do you say God is, then?"

I was recently asked this question by a student bristling at the idea that anyone, let alone a church pastor wedded to outdated ideas, could claim to have an answer worth hearing.

A wonderful opportunity no doubt, but where to start? As I prepared to answer, it struck me that the question itself can become almost paralysing because there are so many potential directions in which we *could* go. Of course, there are many good places from which we could start, but in a society in which the very word 'god' is becoming increasingly privatised and personally-defined, so that it is almost devoid of consistent meaning, *where* we start seems to take on unprecedented importance. We can speak of God all we want, but unless our hearers are clear as to *which* God we mean, and what he is like, we will struggle to make ourselves understood. How are we to give an account of God which does justice to him as he really is?

The way in which we answer that question also has ramifications well beyond evangelism and apologetics. In every element of pastoral ministry, from outreach, to 1-to-1 counselling, to small-group ministry, to preaching, our goal must be to see worshippers turn from idols to worship the true and living God (1 Thess 1:9). At every point we are creatures looking to re-orientate ourselves and our fellow creatures towards our Creator.

Consider your pastoral conversations this week. Inevitably, each of them boils down to how we lead people back to the God of the Bible in light of their anxieties, misunderstandings, or attachment to the world and its desires. Ultimately this means that all pastoral ministry is rooted in our account of who God is.

In this article we are particularly going to focus on how central the Creator-creature distinction is to our view of God in pastoral ministry. We will begin by examining the way it is essential to our understanding of God and our place in the world. Next, we will consider how this shapes our understanding of sin and idolatry, and what the gospel provides. Finally, we will explore the difference that the Creator-creature distinction makes 'on the ground' in pastoral ministry.

## Humble Creatures

Scripture itself opens with a fundamental assumption about reality: "In the beginning, God..." (Gen 1:1a). Before the beginning had been begun, before all other existence was, God was. This is a crucial distinction. There was a time when I was not. There was a time when everything else was not. But there was never a time when God was not. As such, he is the foundation and source of all reality, the basis for all that exists.

Christian theology has long proclaimed this as the fundamental distinction without which it is impossible to claim true knowledge of God, ourselves, or anything else in all reality. It is precisely here that Calvin famously begins his *Institutes*:

John Calvin, *Institutes*, 1.1.1 (emphasis added).

*Nearly all the wisdom we possess, that is to say, true and sound wisdom, consists of two parts: the knowledge of God and of ourselves. But, while joined by many bonds, which one precedes and brings forth the other is not easy to discern. In the first place, no one can look upon himself without immediately turning his thoughts to the contemplation of God, "in whom he lives and moves" (Acts 17:8). For, quite clearly, the mighty gifts with which we are endowed are hardly from ourselves;* **indeed, our very being is nothing but subsistence in the one God***.*

Calvin does not begin with humanity as the ultimate starting point. Rather, his starting point is the two planes of existence; on the one hand, uncreated, eternal and infinite; on the other, created, temporal and finite. Given this fundamental distinction, it becomes clear that everything that we are, all our human faculties, even our very existence, is entirely dependent on the uncreated Creator.

Given that our goal in pastoral ministry is to engage ourselves and others in right worship, this should excite us. It is the very reason we find all creation declaring God to be worthy of worship:

**Rev 4:11**

*"You are worthy, our Lord and God, to receive glory and honour and power, for you created all things, and by your will they were created and have their being."*

As John is presented with a vision of the throne room of God in all holiness, of the highest angelic beings constantly declaring "Holy, Holy, Holy," he hears this cry of praise to God centring on the distinction between God and creation. The startling fact prompting praise is that God *willed* everything to exist, and unless he had done this nothing at all would exist besides God himself. You and I, pastors and those they pastor, everyone and everything, exist only because God *wills* us to.

This is profoundly humbling. We live in a world which prizes human independence. We raise children to become independent thinkers, able to live independent lives. Society prizes personal autonomy over almost any other ethical or social principle. Meanwhile we live in fear of what is to come when old age and infirmity bring dependence on others. We devote more and more resources to stave off the inevitable, and increasingly people speak of the right to end their lives prematurely when 'the burden of dependence' is too great. The Creator-creature distinction speaks into all this fervent activity with an arresting dose of spiritual reality: Human independence, so highly prized, is an illusion. There is no one who is not entirely dependent on their Creator for everything. "He himself gives everyone life and breath and everything else" (Acts 17:25).

This is crucial for pastoral ministry. As we engage in the work of calling worshippers to turn from idols to the true and living God, the question lurks: "why is *this* God worthy of worship?" The Creator-creature distinction provides a significant answer. It is *this* God who is the uncreated Creator. We are created creatures. It is only this God, beyond anyone or anything in the universe, who exists not according to the will of another, but simply because of his aseity, his own self-existence. This staggering gulf between Creator and creature is precisely the reason he is worthy of creation's worship.

## Honoured Images

Although we are rightly humbled by this, pausing to consider God's worth as Creator in this way also brings the profound dignity and honour of our position as the 'highest' of creatures into focus. As human beings we were created in "the image" and "likeness" of no less than *this* Creator (Gen 1:26-27). In short, by creating us in his image, God has given humanity the highest possible place open to a creature.

The depths of this truth about humanity cannot be overestimated. Understanding our 'creatureliness' correctly will both raise our sense of dignity and ensure that we think of ourselves soberly. As images, we are conferred royal status in God's creation as his representatives. We are even made vice-regents, ruling on behalf of the Creator King himself. This means that humanity is lifted above the rest of creation in worth and dignity.

However, while this is certainly a high calling, these heights are not unlimited. The creation account also maintains that humans remain rooted within creation itself. For example, just as the rest of creation, humans are made according to a spoken act of God (albeit a unique one). Similarly, humans are made alongside animals on day 6 of the Genesis account. Francis Schaeffer concludes:

Francis A. Schaeffer and Udo W. Middelmann, *Pollution and the Death of Man* (Wheaton, Ill.: Crossway, 2011), 50.

*As a Christian I say, "Who am I?" Am I only the hydrogen atom, the energy particle extended? No, I am made in the image of God. I know who I am. Yet, on the other hand, when I turn around and face nature, I face something that is like myself. I, too, am created, just as the animal and the plant and the atom are created.*

This is all very well, but as we press into the truth of the Creator-creature distinction, it may feel like we are in danger of becoming the worst kind of theologians, speaking in lofty terms unconnected to the real lives we engage with daily. What does this really have to do with our everyday pastoral ministry? You can imagine the response: "Never mind this theological jargon. Whatever God created people to be, they are sinners now and they need to hear about Jesus. Just get on with it!" And yet, the reality of sin and our need for Jesus is just where the Creator-creature distinction proves so valuable.

## <u>Proud Rebels Reaching for More</u>

For reflection on this, see especially the articles by Graham Beynon and Tim Ward in *Primer* issue 02.

We tend to define 'sin' in various ways. Rebellion, disobedience, pride, idolatry and more. Each description offers its own perspective on the state of sinful hearts towards God, and the subsequent salvation work of Christ in overcoming sin. It is powerful to note, however, that an antagonism towards the Creator-creature distinction lies at the centre of each. The impulse to ignore the inherent authority of the Creator leads to rebellion and disobedience. Similarly, the impulse to dissolve the distinction between creature and Creator entirely is evident in both pride and idolatry. On the one hand, human pride attempts to raise humanity up to the Creator's level. On the other, idolatry seeks to reduce God to a controllable and limited creature. As Geerhardus Vos puts it:

Geerhardus Vos, *Reformed dogmatics* (ed. Richard B Gaffin; vol. 2: Anthropology; Bellingham, WA: Lexham Press, 2012), 51.

*We find the essence of sin in general to be this: that man (1) divorces himself and his relationships from God; (2) places them as a separate center in opposition to God; (3) makes them act against God.*

Sin's 'target' is nothing less than the Creator-creature distinction itself.

This should not surprise us when we consider Genesis 3. What was it that was so tempting to Adam and Eve? "For God knows that when you eat from it your eyes will be opened, and you will be like God, knowing good and evil" (Gen 3:5). The enticing draw was the prospect of being *like God*.

The tragic irony of this is, of course, heightened by the fact that this encounter with temptation comes only a couple of pages after the wonder of human creation in God's image. Humanity already enjoys what the serpent offers.

Ultimately, the combination which we have already noted, of creaturely limitation and dignity, is precisely what sinful humanity strikes against. We reach for something beyond our created status as 'mere' images, wanting to take God's role for ourselves, as though we were the 'original' itself. Even as we do we find ourselves falling short of the heights for which we were made. In the end the prospect of independence, of self-governing authority and power, of autonomy, proved enough for humanity to attempt to overthrow our created place and wrestle against the foundation of reality and existence itself. If only we had been content with our place as creatures, with the combination of limitation and honour that brings! What shame it should cause as we consider our inclination to strain against the distinction between ourselves and our Creator! As Aslan reminds Prince Caspian:

> **"** *You come of the Lord Adam and the Lady Eve... And that is both honour enough to erect the head of the poorest beggar, and shame enough to bow the shoulders of the greatest emperor on earth. Be content.*

C. S. Lewis, *Prince Caspian* (London: Lion, 1989), 185.

In human sin, therefore, the Creator-creature distinction became tragically distorted. The freedom of created reality was twisted and viewed as restrictive, and humanity fell far short of our high status, even as we tried to reach beyond it.

What does this mean for pastoral ministry? Simply put, at the heart of every person we meet is a self-defeating hostility towards the Creator-creature distinction. A.W. Tozer puts it this way:

> **"** *Whatever else the Fall may have been, it was certainly a sharp change in man's relation to his Creator. He adopted toward God an altered attitude, and by so doing destroyed the proper Creator-creature relation in which, unknown to him, his true happiness lay. Essentially salvation is the restoration of a right relation between man and his Creator, a bringing back to normal of the Creator-creature relation.*

A. W. Tozer, *The Pursuit of God* (Milton Keynes, Bucks: Authentic Media, 2004), 67.

In other words, the gospel has *everything* to do with the Creator-creature distinction. The problem the gospel solves is the problem of the distorted Creator-creature distinction.

The impulse

to ignore

the inherent

authority of

the Creator

leads to

rebellion and

disobedience.

# Identity and Idolatry

When we recognise the degree of antagonism to the Creator-creature distinction at the heart of human sin, we also start to see why sin is so corrosive to human identity. Since the Creator-creature distinction is inherent to what it means to be created in the image of God, it is also central in defining what a human actually is. In turn, this means that a strike against the Creator is also a strike against our very selves as creatures and images. Sin ultimately *dehumanises* us as we become images untethered from our Creator, the 'original' to which we owe our very existence.

This is surely why we find the impulse towards idolatry so strong for those we encounter in pastoral ministry, as well as for ourselves. As images, humans are designed to depend on *something* for a stable sense of identity. Distorting the Creator-creature distinction undermines the central relationship which provides that stability but does not negate the need for it. Hence, sinful humans are left scrabbling to reconstruct identities for themselves, precisely the dynamic Isaiah notes as his people turn towards idolatry:

> *Isa 41:6*
>
> *The metalworker encourages the goldsmith, and the one who smooths with the hammer spurs on the one who strikes the anvil. One says of the welding, 'It is good.' The other nails down the idol so that it will not topple.*

Notice the ironic echoes of God's declaration over creation in the words, "it is good!" as idol-makers lift themselves to the place of Creator. Meanwhile their attempts to create stability are pathetic as they "nail down" their pitiful idols to avoid them falling over. Rather than humbly receiving their creaturely identity through the declaration of their Creator, these idol-makers attempt to 'self-create' an identity which they can define and therefore control. The echoes of Genesis 3 are almost deafening.

Little wonder that when reflecting on the persistent idolatry exhibited in the Old Testament, Calvin remarks that, "man's nature... is a perpetual factory of idols." It is important to note Calvin's description of the *reasons* for this:

>
>
> *Calvin, Institutes, 1.11.8.*
>
> *Man's mind, full as it is of pride and boldness, dares to imagine a god according to its own capacity; as it sluggishly plods, indeed is overwhelmed with the crassest ignorance, it conceives an unreality and an empty appearance as God.*

The impulse towards idolatry exhibits human pride, lifting ourselves up and bringing God down to our "own capacity" to understand and control. Ultimately, we have opposed the Creator-creature distinction to such a degree that we have "exchanged the truth about God for a lie, and worshipped and served created things rather than the Creator" (Rom 1:25).

# Humanity Re-placed

What happens, then, when we encounter the salvation offered in Christ? Sinners are brought face-to-face with unfathomable grace. Rebels are brought face-to-face with their all-powerful Lord. Creatures are brought face-to-face with their Creator. Dehumanised creatures, untethered from their source of existence and identity, can find their proper place and true identity in the created order as restored images of God.

We know that, in the physical realm, proper order depends on the right relationships of things relative to one another. In 2018 the thrilling-sounding General Conference on Weights and Measures moved to change the definition of the kilogram. Since 1889 the kilogram itself was defined by the weight of a platinum-alloy cylinder called *Le Grand K* (or LGK). The problem was that LGK had deteriorated over time leading to a lessening in its weight by roughly the weight of a human eyelash. That might seem imperceptible, but since all other weights were defined by it, every other measurement of weight in the world became slightly inaccurate as LGK shifted. In a scientific environment dependent on absolutely precise measurements, a new standard had to be found. The right relationships of weights and measurements to one another requires a fixed point from which to begin.

What we perhaps forget is that this is also true for everything in the created realm, physical or not. We are frequently defined according to the relationships we have with other people and things. I am a husband because I am married to my wife, a father because there are six children for whom that is true. I am able to type these words onto a laptop because my relationship with it is one of worker and tool. In order to correctly measure and inhabit all of our relationships with everything and everyone, let alone all other relationships between everyone and everything, we also require a fixed starting point from which to begin measuring. Tozer puts it this way,

> *In determining relationships we must begin somewhere. There must be somewhere a fixed center against which everything else is measured, where the law of relativity does not enter and we can say "IS" and make no allowances. Such a center is God.*

Tozer, *The Pursuit of God*, 68.

This is the benefit of a ministry that holds onto the Creator-creature distinction. We proclaim access in Christ to the unchanging God. In relationship with him, we have a stable identity. Everything else changes. Every other relationship ebbs and flows. Every other role we have evolves or ends. But the wonderful news of pastoral ministry in the Creator-creature distinction is that our humanity finds its true and secure place in relation to its Creator.

We proclaim

access in

Christ to the

unchanging

God. In

relationship

with him, we

have a stable

identity.

## Pastoring in the Distinction

The final question then, is how this actually works in life and ministry. What does this right awareness of the Creator-creature distinction – that "I am not God, you are not God, they are not God, but God is God" – actually do in the nitty-gritty of life? We might look for answers by imagining a morning spent meeting with a couple of church members.

### Meet James

In the midst of an intensely busy week, the morning begins as a young Christian comes to see us after mentioning that he has been struggling with one or two things lately. James has been relatively successful so far in his life, is outgoing and appears to have a number of good friends, which means that it's a surprise when he reveals his emotional struggles. He reports consistently feeling low. There is no apparent specific ongoing sin in his life, yet he deeply lacks assurance of his salvation, and has a consistently negative view of himself and is experiencing deep spiritual depression. As we begin to explore his account of God, what might we find? There could be multiple points which might prompt us to explore further, but in this instance imagine his lack of assurance leads you to inquire about his understanding of God's love.

*"Well I know he's my heavenly Father who loves me. I know that I'm forgiven because Jesus died for me, but it makes me sad that I constantly let him down. I'm sad that I disappoint him and make him sad. He loves me so much, why would I respond like that?"*

What are we to make of James' account of God? There is much here that is wonderfully right and good. He is certain of forgiveness because of Christ's death and aware of his adoption to sonship (Eph 1:5). He is rightly concerned about ongoing sin and wants to turn away from it to please his Heavenly Father. But what *sort* of father has he in mind? His conception of God as Heavenly Father sounds a lot like a limited human father writ large. This is a father who discovers things about him, and is deeply disappointed, a father whose love is responsive and fluctuates in time.

Now consider the Creator-creature distinction. God is not simply a bigger version of humanity. Human fatherhood is named after God's fatherhood, but that does not mean the analogy works in the other direction, so that we can read what God must be like from our experience of human fathers – idealised or real. In fact, the Creator-creature distinction prompts us to be wary of doing just that. In contrast, we are brought to see a deep distinction between human creaturely love and divine Creator love which will speak right into James' account of God.

As we talk then, we might bring to mind the eternality and omniscience of God in distinction to us. All our love, including the love of a father for his children, is necessarily *responsive* (as we discover more about the object of our love) and also *sequential* (as we experience moment by moment interaction with those we love). But God's love is neither of those things. We might remind James of the wonderful promise that he will experience God drawing near to him in love and forgiveness as he turns from sin in repentance and faith (Jam 4:8). At the same time, James can also rest in the Creator-creature distinction. God's eternal nature teaches us to understand his love to be timeless, not simply in the sense of enduring for all time, but in the sense that it exists beyond time itself and the sequential experience of it. No moment, no new knowledge, no new act on our behalf can surprise the Creator who so sets his love on his people. In fact, James is in danger of raising himself up too high, as though he can influence God in such a way, while bringing God lower to the level of a limited creature. Encouragement to recognise the distinction between Creator and creature here can have a re-humanising effect as James sees himself re-placed as an object of this infinite divine love.

## Meet Mary

Later in the same morning we head out for a meeting with another church member. Mary is a busy mother of three teenagers, and we're meeting her in a morning break during work. Her longstanding struggles with significant anxiety have recently deteriorated and are beginning to encroach on her daily life, so she has asked for prayer and help.

It becomes clear that there are two major sources of anxiety. First, the growing independence of her teenage children leads to worry about their safety. The oldest recently learnt to drive, which has taken away the burden of being 'parent-taxi' but it has compounded her anxiety as imagined car crashes and other catastrophes crowd unwanted into her mind while her children are out. Meanwhile, Mary feels pressure to increase her work hours now that her department know her youngest is at secondary school. She is concerned that her colleagues are growing resentful. Just the day before we meet, she had delivered a presentation to a room of decidedly bored looking faces. She hates to imagine what they must have been thinking.

Once again, consider the Creator-creature distinction. It may not be immediately clear how Mary's account of God is at play, until we begin to consider her account of *herself*. What degree of knowledge is she claiming for herself? Catastrophising contains a 'fortune-telling' element, a thought process which claims to know certain outcomes should certain events take place. Similarly, the anxieties which she faces concerning her colleagues exhibit the cognitive distortion of 'mind-reading' based on presumed knowledge of others which she simply doesn't have as a finite creature. Some of the roots of her anxiety are firmly sunk into a raising up of herself – and her knowledge in particular – towards the level only her omniscient Creator can inhabit. Meanwhile this uncovers a diminished view of God in both his sovereignty and goodness towards her. It may be unintentional, but her responses to a fallen and frustrated world strain against the Creator-creature distinction, and she needs to be gently encouraged that, "you are not God, they are not God. God is God." The wonderful hope is that as Mary responds to a restored relationship with her Creator, she may yet experience the re-humanising effect of diminished anxiety.

## Resting in the Distinction

With these two pastoral encounters, our morning comes to an end. Both have been emotionally demanding, and both have inevitably taken just a little more time than we had either hoped or planned. Perhaps as we pray with Mary before arranging to catch up at a future date we're already beginning to feel the pressure of the rest of this week's jobs piling up. The agenda for that leaders' meeting needs to be drawn up. Then there's the Bible study tomorrow and Joan to visit in hospital. And Sunday has a habit of coming around every week doesn't it?

Pastoral ministry is never finished, and there is always more that could be done. Which means that the Creator-creature distinction is absolutely vital for the way we see *ourselves* in pastoral ministry, just as much as for others. My days off each week are often marked by a feeling of frustration and irritability. All too often the reason is that once again I haven't managed to do the ten or so days' worth of work I've been attempting since the last day off. How often in pastoral ministry we wish we were more than we are, with more time and power than we have!

For a final time though, consider the Creator-creature distinction. Although all work including pastoral ministry is frustrated since the fall, the root of my day off frustration is *not* my fallenness. It is, instead, my sinful reaction to creatureliness. In a repeat of Gen 3, I find myself frustrated at my limitations. I struggle for yet more productivity in a vain attempt to escape them. As a creature in my Creator's image, I need to be reminded that I am limited by nature, and that as part of the "very good" creation.

Meanwhile, I can rest in the infinite nature of our Creator who cannot be limited. He is the omnipotent, eternal, infinite one. As creatures in his image, we have the honour of representing him to the rest of creation. As those in pastoral ministry, we have the honour of doubly representing him in our calling as "Christ's ambassadors" (2 Cor 5:20). However, forget our place in the Creator-creature distinction and this high honour becomes an intolerable and dehumanising burden. We are not called to change James or Mary, or anyone else ourselves. We are not called to devote unlimited time, energy and knowledge to those under our care. Rather, we are called to rest in reliance on our Creator and all-powerful Saviour to do *his* work through us. And there is nothing more re-humanising than that!

## Questions for further thought and discussion

The Personal-Infinite God

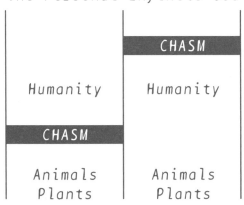

1. How does this diagram capture what Matt's described from Genesis? (adapted from Francis Schaeffer's book *The God Who is There*)

   Why are both the left and the right sides the diagram important? Which do you think needs more emphasis today and why?

2. Alongside James and Mary, what other struggles in the Christian life do you think could be helped by a stronger grasp of who God is and the Creator-creature distinction?

3. What has most humbled/amazed/comforted you as you've read this issue of *Primer*?

"The reason why God has no passions is that passions imply passivity and intermission. The passion of love is something that happens to us, as 'getting wet' happens to a body: and God is exempt from that 'passion' in the same sense that water is exempt from 'getting wet.' He cannot be affected with love, because he *is* love."

C S Lewis, *Miracles*